I0126784

Quarterly Essay

CONTENTS

Quarterly Essay is published four times a year by Black Inc., an imprint of Schwartz Publishing Pty Ltd. Publisher: Morry Schwartz.

ISBN 9781863954013 ISSN 1832-0953

Subscriptions (4 issues): $49 a year within Australia incl. GST (Institutional subs. $59). Outside Australia $79. Payment may be made by Mastercard, Visa or Bankcard, or by cheque made out to Schwartz Publishing. Payment includes postage and handling.

To subscribe, fill out and post the subscription card, or subscribe online at:

www.quarterlyessay.com

Correspondence and subscriptions should be addressed to the Editor at:

Black Inc.
Level 5, 289 Flinders Lane
Melbourne VIC 3000 Australia
Phone: 61 3 9654 2000
Fax: 61 3 9654 2290
Email:
quarterlyessay@blackincbooks.com (editorial)
subscribe@blackincbooks.com (subscriptions)

Editor: Chris Feik
Management: Sophy Williams
Production Co-ordinator: Caitlin Yates
Publicity: Anna Lensky
Design: Guy Mirabella

BIPOLAR NATION

How to Win the 2007 Election

Peter Hartcher

A type of market research called the projective technique, long applied in the consumer products field, is now coming to be used in politics. It's supposed to be a way of delving beneath consumers' surface responses to get to their deeper, unarticulated feelings. They are asked to "project" their feelings for one thing onto another.

So, for example, in the prelude to the last US presidential election, market researchers asked Americans to think about their presidential candidates as cars. If George W. Bush were a car, what make would he be? The most common answer was that he'd be a Ford. And his opponent, Senator John Kerry? He'd be a BMW.

What does it mean? A Ford is nothing glamorous. But it is genuine local product, familiar and reliable. A BMW is expensive and high-performance. But it is foreign, elitist and European. Suspiciously European. It's no surprise, on this analysis, that Bush went on to win the 2004 election.

In Australia, Tim Grau of the public-affairs consultancy Springboard conducted a similar exercise in 2005. He asked voters in focus groups to think of our national leaders as dogs. If John Howard were a dog, what breed would he be?

The most common answers were fox terrier, bulldog and Jack Russell terrier. What does this mean? "Our research has consistently found that strong and successful political leaders are characterised by voters as 'worker' dogs," reported Grau, "the type you would have for protection or to do work around the home or property". They are small, agile and aggressive.

Asked the same question about Peter Costello, voters most commonly replied that he'd be a labrador or cocker spaniel. These, said Grau, are the sorts of breeds you might like to play with in the backyard, but not the sorts of dogs you would trust to protect your house and family.

When it came to the former Opposition leader Kim Beazley, by far the most common reaction was Saint Bernard, followed by Great Dane. These breeds are supposed to be likeable and loyal; the bad news is that they are also seen as big, cuddly, slow and dopey – not the types you'd trust with the protection of the family home.

Although Grau once worked for the Labor Party, his findings carry a favourable implication for Howard – voters see him as the ideal breed for leadership.

What about Kevin Rudd? He was not included in the exercise, conducted when he was merely a frontbencher. In early 2007, voters were still forming their impressions of the new Labor leader. Rudd has the qualities that he needs to emerge as a strong, viable alternative prime minister – he is more terrier than labrador – but the open question is whether the electorate will see him that way.

You only get one chance to make a first impression, and Rudd has used his well. Within three months of replacing Beazley, the new Opposition leader's approval rating was a very strong 60 per cent, double Beazley's terminal performance and a full twenty points ahead of Howard's rating according to Newspoll. He had also lifted Labor's share of the primary vote by a remarkable seven or eight percentage points and put it in a commanding position.

Rudd casts Australia's choice as one between a stale government and a refreshed Labor Party; between a government of market fundamentalists and a Labor Party of social fairness; between a Prime Minister who runs the country on hour-by-hour political spin and a Labor leader of steady long-term purpose.

Rudd has drawn several constituencies. First are the disheartened voters who had drifted leftwards, away from Labor to the Greens and elsewhere. They have taken heart from Rudd's ideological eloquence. Their hope in Labor has been rekindled by his clarity and idealism in setting out a social-democratic alternative to what Rudd has called "Howard's Brutopia".

This group of recovering Labor voters had given up on Beazley as just a windy reiteration of Howardism and they are intrigued by Rudd's promise to be "an alternative, not an echo". In a privatised era when it seems no one will defend the role of the state in society, Rudd is not afraid to say that the resources of the state should be mobilised in the systematic support of the vulnerable. He has argued strongly for more public invest-ment in education as a key public good. And his own life story seems to tell us that he really means it. He has told of how his family was evicted from its tenant farm when his father died. And of how he was able to work his way from a poor start in rural Queensland into Australia's dip-lomatic service thanks to Whitlam's gift of free university education.

It must be said that Rudd's articulate intellectualism titillates some on the left. When Howard gave his ideologically triumphant address to a *Quadrant* dinner in October last year celebrating the death of "philo-communism" and the struggle against "political correctness", there was a quiescent silence from Beazley. It seemed there would be no reply from Labor until, a month later, Rudd published an intellectual response in *The Monthly*. "Ideas matter", a Rudd refrain, appeals to an educated elite which delights in seeing politics waged not only in sound-grabs but also as a contest of ideology.

Another group of voters from the political right is interested in his unapologetic Christianity and his critique of Howard from a conservative standpoint. Rudd accuses Howard of betraying the Liberals' Menzian tradition and of crossing the line, going "a bridge too far" in pursuit of an extremist neo-liberal agenda, notably with his WorkChoices laws. Howard, says Rudd, has broken the "social contract" that has held Australia together for a century.

It is striking that the Australian political tradition he has chosen to champion in this cause is not that of any Labor leader, but that of the patrician Sir Robert Gordon Menzies, founder of the Liberal Party and John Howard's declared hero. Rudd associates himself with Menzies' "responsible conservatism and social liberalism", portraying Howard as a traitor to the traditions of his own party. Rudd wants to drive a wedge between two planks of conservative thinking, characterising Howard as a neo-liberal, neo-conservative fundamentalist who has betrayed the social conservatism of the Menzian mainstream. Rudd will restore it and "recover the middle ground".

I was so struck by this unabashed embrace of the Liberals' founder that I asked the new Labor leader if he was Australia's modern Menzies. Rudd did not seek to disavow him. He said Menzies, in the tradition of the nineteenth-century British conservative Benjamin Disraeli, understood that there was a social contract, "a set of obligations binding those who have power to those who have none".

> Menzies came from that tradition. Menzies engaged in other forms of destructive legislation, which I don't need to elaborate, but Menzies came from that tradition. Menzies would be turning in his grave to see the fabric of the current industrial relations legislation. Howard is stepping radically outside the longstanding liberal mainstream tradition in this country.

Thirdly, Rudd has drawn the interest of the political centre. This is partly out of simple relief that he is not Kim Beazley. Sometime last year, through the mysterious osmotic process by which millions of people arrive at the same conclusion at around the same time, Australians simply closed their ears to Beazley. A Nicholson animation in the last week of Beazley's tenure showed him talking the leg off a wooden stool. Rudd, with his deputy, Julia Gillard, arrived fresh. However briefly, the collective ear opened. Rudd won our attention.

It is partly because many had watched Rudd in his five years as Labor's foreign affairs spokesman and been impressed with his calm but relentless prosecutorial pursuit of John Howard and Alexander Downer across the deserts of Iraq, through the cells of Guantánamo, down the hallways of the White House and between the silos of the AWB.

It is partly because we see that Rudd is not just the latest product to fall from the conveyor of the clanking Labor machine, but his own man. He has never worked in a union or as a party apparatchik. He does not owe his ascendancy to a faction. He is one of the few federal Labor MPs who does not enjoy the patronage of a major union. And he is not the product of a Labor family dynasty. So when he formed his frontbench, the factions were shut out of the decision of whom he would choose. And when he took the leadership, he announced that he would no longer attend meetings of his faction, the Right. This makes Rudd unique in the annals of modern Labor.

It is partly because Rudd emerged as a strong voice speaking for a concerned mainstream on the urgent new priority of global warming. This issue moved from the periphery to the centre of Australian politics so quickly and decisively that Howard has had to scramble to try to keep up. While the Prime Minister has been unconvincingly attempting to reposition himself from sceptic to saviour, Rudd has been a clear and articulate advocate. Howard's famous political antennae failed him on global warming, and Rudd was ready while Howard fumbled.

It is partly because, although Rudd has been a tough critic of the government, he seems to offer more than the customary oppositionism. He isn't seen to be just whining about the government. He seems to offer an optimistic alternative. This is where the shrewd and expensive Labor decision to help shape public perceptions of Rudd with an early TV ad campaign paid off. With the verdant Queensland bush behind him and the twang of a steel-stringed guitar accompanying him, Rudd began with a folksy, "This is the part of country Australia where my parents raised me." He had a call to abandon complacency: "Some call us the lucky country, but I believe you make your own luck. We can't just hope that the resources boom lasts forever." He had a positive plan for our kids' future that he contrasted with Howard's WorkChoices: "Australia must now plan for an education revolution boosting early childhood, schools, tech colleges, universities – and insisting on higher standards so that Australia can take on the world through the best trained people, not by cutting wages and conditions."

It is partly because we might even see in Kevin Rudd a younger version of what we saw in John Howard. A politician, yes, but an ordinary-looking bloke who talks sensibly to common concerns about mainstream issues. He is not alien to the mainstream, like Paul Keating, and he doesn't seem in any way erratic, like Mark Latham. He even has Howard's glasses and grey hair.

So, arriving fresh, and apparently drawing support from the left, right and centre of the electorate, Rudd built very strong support very quickly, according to the polls. The most extraordinary poll finding was the 12 February 2007 report that Kevin Rudd had built the highest approval rating of any Opposition leader in the thirty-five years of the ACNielsen. His approval rating of 64 per cent was almost messianic. It made him more popular than Bob Hawke at his folk-hero peak just before he swept Malcolm Fraser from power in 1983.

This, of course, is the very definition of a honeymoon. If you take the polls as a statement of voting intention, you are seriously misled. For Rudd Labor to lead the government by 56 per cent to 44 per cent on a two-party preferred basis – the February Newspoll result – means that, statistically, the Coalition's odds of winning are less than one in 10,000, according to the probability analysis of Andrew Leigh, an economist and poll-watcher at the Australian National University. He thinks that the odds offered at the online betting agency Centrebet on the same day, 6 February 2007, are a better indicator of the electoral outlook – they showed a Labor win paying $1.90, meaning that Labor had a 49 per cent chance of victory.

What the polls were really telling us was that Rudd has our attention. Remember that Mark Latham had a similarly strong poll rating during his honeymoon, yet he delivered Labor its worst election result in seventy years. The polls are a snapshot, not a predictor. Now that Rudd has the nation's attention, we will watch and listen and draw our conclusions in the months ahead. Walter Mondale, US vice-president under Jimmy Carter, once remarked that "political image is like mixing cement; when it's wet, you can move it around and shape it, but at some point it hardens and there is almost nothing you can do to reshape it." For Rudd, the cement is still wet early in election year 2007.

Tim Grau is not the first person to compare a federal leader to a canine. Jeff Kennett once disparaged Peter Costello as having "all the attributes of a dog – except loyalty". Categorising our national leaders as varieties of dog is irreverent, cheeky, and that's why audiences love to hear about it – greying industrialists and grave-faced economists every bit as much as flip undergraduates and the anxious unemployed. In talks that I give to various audiences on national politics, it never fails to raise a gleeful laugh. We delight in taking down our leaders. They are all just a pack of dogs, as one big investor put it to me. The more we belittle our leaders, the more we enjoy ourselves.

The historian John Hirst believes that Australian egalitarianism explains this phenomenon: "So that all men can be equal, politicians have to be dishonoured." He traces our national disdain for our politicians to the 1850s, when London decided to allow the Australian colonies to give the vote to a much broader segment of the population. "Respect for Parliament evaporated very quickly" with the arrival of this more democratic era, writes Hirst in his book *Sense & Nonsense in Australian History*.

He recounts the story of how the NSW chief justice in 1861 shared a joke about politicians with a criminal on trial in his court, the highest and lowest reaches of society conspiring to make fun of their elected leaders. The accused, on trial for escaping from gaol, was worried that the chief justice might not have an open mind in his case because he had been the same judge who had sent him to gaol on the original charge. He wanted a new judge to hear his case. The chief justice, said the accused, might have "prejudicial feelings" against him. The judge misheard and, thinking that the crook had spoken of "political feelings", enquired: "Why should I have political feelings against you? Are you a member of Parliament?" The crook replied: "Not yet."

Although a member of a reviled group, a leader's standing is nevertheless vital, especially if that leader happens to be prime minister. Fascinating new research by Professor Ian McAllister of the Australian National University has shown that every extra percentage point in a prime minister's approval rating produces an improvement of 0.47 of a percentage point in the government's electoral support compared with that of the opposition. So a prime minister with a strong approval rating can lift the electability of his entire party – he is a political strongman who, for every step he moves up in our esteem, is able to raise his party by a half-step. And, again, Howard has proved to be a breed apart. His approval rating has turned out to be the most enduringly buoyant in the thirty-year history of opinion polling in Australia. Paul Keating, in his five years as prime minister, rarely moved out of the 30 per cent approval range. Howard has never been in it. Most Australians approve of the way Howard does his job, most of the time, according to both the main published opinion polls, Newspoll and ACNielsen.

Opposition leaders don't make so much of a difference. The standing of a prime minister is almost three times more powerful than that of an Opposition leader in deciding elections, McAllister found. An extra percentage point in an Opposition leader's approval rating produces an advantage against the government of only 0.18 per cent.

So a leader's standing matters a great deal. His breed characteristics, his polled approval rating – however you want to measure it, the way that the voters rate leaders is a vital variable in deciding the outcome of our country's political equation.

But on what basis do we rate our leaders? How do we make a judgment about their standing? Is it based on their personality? It is, of course, in part. We are human and we have human responses to others. It is undeniable that some Australians voted for Bob Hawke because of his irresistible sex appeal; I know one who said she did so simply because of his mesmerisingly lovely, silvery, wavy mane of hair. Others voted for Paul Keating because of his air of dashing dangerousness. This is an element of the political contest that seems to have become dormant in the age of John Howard, a man whom Michelle Grattan once memorably described as "awesomely ordinary". Labor's national secretary, Tim Gartrell, unable to unseat the Prime Minister, resorted instead to satirising him as "a 21st-century cross between Richard Nixon and Gollum from *Lord of the Rings*".

Yet leaders' personalities and personal attributes are thoroughly inadequate as a way of explaining how Australians vote. If we voted according to our reactions to leaders' personal qualities, Kim Beazley would have defeated Howard for the prime ministership. How can we know this?

In the 2001 Australian Electoral Study, rigorous and wide-ranging polling conducted by the political science departments of some of the country's leading universities, Howard and Beazley were seen to be about equally intelligent, knowledgeable and inspiring. But on three other positive personality attributes, Beazley was seen as the better candidate – more honest than Howard, more trustworthy and more compassionate. Howard had an edge on Beazley on two measures – he was seen to be a fraction more sensible and, in the only area where he had a commanding lead on his rival, he was seen as offering "strong leadership" by a margin of 72 per cent to Beazley's 45 per cent.

Anyone arriving in Australia from Mars and being shown this polling could have been excused for predicting that Beazley was likely to win an electoral contest. Voters' reactions to Howard's personality were hardly warm: he had a decisive advantage over Beazley in only one of the eight positive personal attributes. But Howard was preferred overwhelmingly on the question of "strong leadership". So if we are not responding to Howard's personality so much as to his leadership, how are we forming these views?

By the time of the election expected this year, Howard will have been in power for about twelve years. This is one-fifth of the entire span of the modern Australian two-party political system, which took shape in 1949 with Robert Menzies' creation of the Liberal Party. This is a remarkable endurance.

At every election, John Howard reminds us in the starkest possible terms that our federal government has the weightiest of responsibilities. The national government has monopoly power over the two areas that most immediately and emphatically determine the fate of the country – macroeconomic management and national security, our prosperity and our security. Strip everything else away, and these are the bedrock policy determinants of national success. Or national failure.

A federal election is where, for the briefest moment, we have the power to choose which party will manage these grave national responsibilities. You may want to snicker at me for the rest of the political cycle, Howard seems to be telling us, but on election day I want you to understand that you are taking part in the highest of high-stakes enterprises for a democratic nation-state. Not only that, Howard seems to say, but I want you to worry about it. And if you're not worried, he will try to make you so.

After winning power in the 1996 "anti-Keating" election, Howard has used one or other of these two themes – national prosperity and national security – to win every election since. In 1998 Howard used the purported danger of Labor to make us fear for our post-recession prosperity; in the post-9/11 election of 2001 he told us to worry about terrorists and suspicious boat people; in 2004 he frightened us with the threats to both our prosperity and our security. Labor, he said, was a danger to our interest rates and also a threat to the US alliance in an age of terror.

This is Howard's formula. He reminds us at every election that the federal government is here to provide prosperity and security, and then frightens us with the thought that either of these could be at risk. And guess what? It just so happens that the Australian voting public sees Labor as being the better party to handle just about every other major area of policy – health, education, industrial relations, welfare, family issues – but not these two great federal monopoly powers. By an emphatic margin of two to one, Australians trust the Howard government to better manage our national prosperity and our national security.

Howard only has a couple of cards to play, but they are the trump cards of Australian national politics.

Kevin Rudd understands this. The Labor leader conceives of Australian politics as a babushka doll that opens, layer upon layer, each time revealing a smaller one inside. In a 2005 interview he put it to me that:

> The outer shell of the babushka doll is national security. The public has to be able to look you in the eye and have confidence that you will maintain security.
>
> Peel that layer off. Next, people want confidence that the economy will be well managed and that you can provide them with the basics of life – a job and an income.

It's only then that the voter will consider what is further within. Rudd continued: "Our experience of the last decade is that the community has had reservations about these two outer shells." Rudd claimed Labor is in the process of recovering public confidence that it can, indeed, be trusted with national security and economic management. He returned to the babushka doll:

> Peel that layer off. Next, people ask, "What will happen if I get sick? Who will be there to look after me?" Next, people want to know,

"How do I provide for my kids' education?" Then, at the inner
core, is community. I think there's still a deep yearning for people
to be involved in community life.

In other words, credibility on the two weighty matters of national "hard
power" – national security and economic management – is a prerequisite
for a political party that hopes to rule the country. Unless the voter can
trust a political party to fulfil the federal responsibilities of security and
prosperity, she will not trust that party with power. As Rudd acknowledged, Labor has lost on these two issues, so it has lost everything.

The respective roles and competencies of the two major parties have
become so deeply imprinted that some politicians and commentators
speculate that they may now be permanent. Bill Bowtell, one-time chief
of staff to Paul Keating, postulates that we differentiate between the political parties' roles as clearly and instinctively as we tell the difference
between Mummy and Daddy.

Mummy and Daddy? American political analysts have sometimes cast
their parties in these gender roles. A Mummy party is most interested in
caring for people. It's empathetic, inclusive and concerned with fairness.
In short, it wants to give you a cuddle. It's seen to be better at providing
services – especially health, education and welfare. A Daddy party, on the
other hand, is strict. It's big on self-discipline and self-reliance. It is frugal
and interested in obedience. In sum, it will stand you on your feet but
keep you on your toes. A Daddy party is trusted to look after the funda-
mentals of keeping the family secure, with good economic management
and strong national security.

In the US, the Democrats are the Mummy party and the Republicans
are the Daddy. "In Australia," Bowtell wrote in the online journal *New
Matilda* in January 2005, "the same applies, but even more so." Labor is our
Mummy party, the Coalition is Daddy. And in Australia, there is a division
of responsibilities between the state and federal levels that follows these

lines of responsibility, these political gender roles. The states are primarily responsible for delivering services – health and education, for instance – while the national government has sole responsibility for national security and macroeconomic management. This helps to explain why Labor has monopolised power at the state level across Australia, while the Coalition has entrenched itself at the federal, according to Bowtell. And he fears that unless Labor can change, it will be forever shut out of power federally:

> In the century since Australian Federation, Labor has formed only two durable national governments – Curtin/Chifley (1941–49) and Hawke/Keating (1983–96). Against type, both these administrations were Daddy governments – facing and taking tough, unpopular decisions in the face of dire threats to national survival and national prosperity.

Unless Labor today can present itself as a credible Daddy party, it will simply fade away as an alternative national government. "Federal Labor is under the grave misapprehension that the people of Australia need it," Bowtell said. In private, some of Australia's most senior and successful Labor politicians concur, but, of course, are reluctant to say so publicly.

Rudd knows and understands this point. Whether he can convincingly cross-dress Labor by late this year remains the dominant question of policy and perception that hangs over the election.

As 2007 opened, Rudd updated his babushka metaphor to incorporate the newly urgent political priority of global warming or, as the Greens call it, "global heating".

A non-issue at the 2004 election, a background subject through most of 2005, global warming had built rapidly towards the end of 2006 and quite suddenly reached critical mass in the mind of the Australian electorate. The first unequivocal evidence of this to emerge publicly was a poll by the Lowy Institute released on 2 October showing that 68 per cent of respondents rated climate change as a "critical threat" to Australia's vital interests over the next ten years, and a bigger danger than Islamic fundamentalism.

This put climate change in the top three perceived threats to the country, behind international terrorism, which was rated as a critical threat by 73 per cent of respondents, and the danger of hostile nations acquiring nuclear weapons, rated by 70 per cent. The next issue on the threat hierarchy after global warming was competition from low-wage countries, gauged to be a critical threat to Australia by only 34 per cent of respondents.

Labor had been talking about the subject for years while the Howard government had been sceptical that man-made global warming was real. But the mounting evidence combined with the crescendo of public concern to change the government's mind.

In a rare and instructive insight into how government works, Alexander Downer described to me the day that he became a climate change convert. It was the weekend after the release of the Lowy Institute poll. Like a good local member, Downer made an appearance between the flower displays and the dog-judging at the Port Elliott Show in his electorate near Adelaide.

"It was a bloody hot day, thirty-three degrees and a north wind – often the Port Elliott Show is cold and rainy," recalled Downer. "And a bunch of people, not just farmers, were saying: 'Maybe there is something in this climate change thing.'"

The Foreign Affairs Minister phoned one of his Liberal colleagues in the Federal Parliament, Greg Hunt, the parliamentary secretary to the minister for the environment and a quiet activist who had spent years advocating the need to act on global warming. "It's time," Downer told him.

For the slight and scholarly Hunt, it was a sweet moment. "He'd been working on me for a long time," confessed Downer. Only a few weeks earlier the pair had thrashed their way through a robust argument on the subject. A hot day in Adelaide turned out to be far more persuasive than a towering stack of scientific papers.

Hunt believes that the conversion of the Howard government was effectively complete on that day, and that Downer was pivotal in helping to change the balance of opinion around the Cabinet table. By the end of the year, only two Cabinet ministers, the Minister for Industry, Ian Macfarlane, and the Minister for Finance, Nick Minchin, remained sceptics on climate change, according to several of their Cabinet colleagues.

Without advertising the fact, the Prime Minister started to immerse himself in research on global warming and policy options in the last months of 2006. He and his ministers commissioned a good deal of work within the bureaucracy. Howard quietly determined to blindside Labor with a new agenda in the year to the next election.

The newly elected Labor leader, Kevin Rudd, moved Peter Garrett into the environment portfolio at the end of 2006 to bring some star power to bear on the subject. Howard responded by deploying some star power of his own, appointing Malcolm Turnbull Minister for the Environment and Water Resources. Howard then opened the political year by announcing a radical $10 billion, ten-year plan to revitalise the atrophying coronary artery of south-eastern Australia, the Murray-Darling river system. It demonstrated that Howard was determined to position himself as an effective environmental problem-solver. A new political battle space had opened up, and John Howard wanted to dominate it.

How does Kevin Rudd position global warming among his assembly of Russian dolls?

> Climate change comes after national security and almost at about the same level of layering as the economy — and before you get to equity and quality of life concerns. Because global warming is a national security matter and an economic matter.

So the new contest is an enlargement of the old. Global warming is not just an environmental matter. It threatens to be an economic cataclysm, with the British economist Nick Stern likening its potential impact to that of the Great Depression and both world wars combined. It is a matter of national security too. This is true in a number of dimensions.

First, it already threatens Australia's supply of fresh water. In February 2007, the fourth assessment report of the Intergovernmental Panel on Climate Change warned that "increases in the amount of precipitation are very likely in high latitudes, while decreases are likely in most subtropical land regions." For Australia, the subtropics is all of the land area south of Rockhampton. In other words, most of the inhabited areas of the country, including every capital city catchment except Darwin's.

Secondly, Oxfam predicts that climate change could put an extra thirty million people at risk of famine. And with more famine comes more disease.

Thirdly, the Pentagon has drawn up a number of plausible confrontations between the world's great powers that could result from global warming. For instance: "Envision Pakistan, India and China – all armed with nuclear weapons – skirmishing at their borders over refugees, access to shared river and arable land." Citing this and other possibilities, the leader of Britain's Conservative Party, David Cameron, has tried to point out that "Climate change is not just an environmental question; it could have a massive impact on national security … Politicians have a duty to prepare for its consequences in terms of domestic and international security." The Tories have proposed annual targets for cutting carbon emissions, just one example of how political parties are mobilising to occupy the new political high ground that this topic has opened up.

In Australia, the shift in thinking has been a long time coming. There is a general perception that protecting the environment is antithetical to preserving a strong economy, that the two exist in direct hostility to each other and that each step forward for one represents a backward step for the other. To preserve a pristine bay, for instance, requires that the proposed oil refinery be denied; saving the whales means bankrupting the Japanese whaling fleet; cutting pollution means inhibiting industry – it is, in short, a zero-sum equation. And, in the absence of lateral solutions, it sometimes proves to be so.

But on the grand scale of civilisational survival, the environmental imperative and the economic need can and must be reconciled. For there is no point in having a gleaming new factory if there is no water to operate it, just as there is no point in having a magnificent view if you can't find work to buy food and shelter.

The encouraging news is that the two public goods – sound economic growth and the preservation of a habitable planet – can be reconciled without any wrenching difficulty. For example, research commissioned by the companies that compose the Australian Business Roundtable on Climate Change suggests that it is possible to cut Australia's greenhouse gas emissions dramatically without imposing any serious cost on economic growth.

According to economic modellers at Monash University, if Australia continues on its present path, carbon emissions will increase by 77 per cent over the next fifty years while the economy will grow by an annual average of 2.2 per cent.

But, if the country were to introduce a well-designed carbon emissions trading system, emissions could be cut by 70 per cent over the same time span, while the economy could grow by a near-identical 2.1 per cent annual average. Is this a magic pudding? A CSIRO policy economist who has worked with the modelling, Dr Steve Hatfield Dodds, said: "It's not so much a magic pudding as long-term, carefully planned structural adjustment."

John Howard sought to draw a moral from this when he announced his $10 billion plan for the rehabilitation of the Murray-Darling river system in January. "Whatever policies we may have, in areas as specific as water security, ultimately, for their effective implementation, they depend upon the continuing strength and growth of the Australian economy," he said at the beginning of his speech. He returned to the subject at the end: "We do not come to this debate unwilling to commit the financial resources of the Commonwealth. Those financial resources are available because ... of the sound economic management of the past decade."

His essential point is that grand-scale environmental problems can only be solved effectively by competent economic managers. Howard will develop this theme. The Prime Minister will try to impose the idea that even if Labor does have a green thumb, it would be all thumbs in managing the great environmental threats of our time.

So there's the rub. The qualifications required to deal with global warming are a reiteration, a repackaging of the abilities required to keep the country prosperous and strong.

To deal with the monumental challenge that climate change poses to the nation's future, will the voting public choose the party that is seen to be marginally more verdant, but threadbare on the economy and national security? Or will Australians prefer to trust the party that they already believe overwhelmingly to be more competent in managing the weightiest responsibilities of the nation-state? Howard hopes and trusts that even with the big environmental problem of our time, it will be a "Come to Daddy" moment for the Australian voter.

Donald Horne's *The Lucky Country*, first published in 1964, was intended as a warning. In the sentence from which the book's title was drawn, he wrote: "Australia is a lucky country run mainly by second-rate people who share its luck." He continued: "It lives on other people's ideas, and although its ordinary people are adaptable, most of its leaders (in all fields) so lack curiosity about the events that surround them that they are often taken by surprise."

The book was a scathing critique of Australia in what Horne called "the Age of Menzies". It damned the country's leadership, its elites, its policies, but never the Australian people.

It's one of the toughest critiques of Australia ever written. Horne's thesis was that Australia's good fortune in the form of mineral wealth had become a prop, an excuse and perhaps even a licence for a terrible national complacency. The nation's luck was its curse.

At its core, Horne said in 2005, the book was "a derivative society thesis – the essential thing in the writing of *The Lucky Country* was derivativeness". And a part of this was an ingrained Australian hostility to originality and to expertise. Horne best captured this idea in a 1976 book, *Money Made Us*:

> Overall, if, with exceptions, there was a scepticism towards original talent, even a hatred of it, the smart thing was to get the design of a proven success from overseas and then follow the instructions on the back of the packet.

The Lucky Country's title passed into the language. The book sold a total of 260,000 copies, utterly extraordinary for an Australian work of non-fiction. It was ranked in the *Sydney Morning Herald*'s Poll of the Century as one of the three most influential Australian books of the twentieth century. The phrase has become synonymous with Australia around the world, and the more widely it has spread, the more widely it has been misunderstood.

For Horne, this was a source of much chagrin: "The long misuse of the phrase 'the lucky country', as if it were praise for Australia rather than a warning, has been a tribute to the empty-mindedness of a mob of assorted public wafflers," he wrote some thirty years later. "When the book first came out people had no doubt the phrase was ironic."

And the warning? Horne warned Australia that its luck was running out. In *The Lucky Country*, Horne detected and foreshadowed Australia's slide from the top ranks of the world's richest countries, arguing that luck and complacency were poor substitutes for originality and investment:

> Australia is playing for a high stake: maintenance of a general level of prosperity higher than almost anywhere in the world. The answer to the question, "Can we keep our standards of prosperity and our present way of life?" or to put it more bluntly, "Can the racket last?" appears to be NO.
>
> That is to say, that if things go on as they are, Australia will slip down the per capita national income scale.

He was, of course, correct, and it was a slippage that gathered pace in the '70s and '80s. When Horne updated the book for its fifth edition in 1998, he was able to insert parenthetically: "Since I wrote these words in the first edition of this book, according to one set of estimates, Australia dropped from fifth to tenth on the list of the world's prosperous countries – in one year."

This is the same phenomenon that the founder of modern Singapore, Lee Kuan Yew, was talking about with his forecast that Australians were destined to become "the poor white trash of Asia".

In 1970, Australian incomes were the fourth highest in the world. In the twenty years that followed, the country's ranking fell inexorably. By 1990 our incomes placed us fifteenth in the world. Other countries surged. Australia stagnated.

We grew accustomed to our condition in the '70s and '80s. We accepted that Asia was rising, that America was towering, but that we were going to have to accept 10 per cent unemployment as our birthright, much as the countries of continental Europe have done. We would have to console ourselves with sunshine and sport, the remnants of our luck. How was Australia ever to emerge from its torpor?

In the last chapter of The Lucky Country, Horne offered three avenues forward for Australia: ways for the country to develop its own identity, to start thinking for itself, to work for its living, and to fulfil its destiny.

The first avenue was to become a republic, the second was to become involved with Asia, and the third was to undertake technological and economic modernisation. In the absence of these three, Horne later said, "Australia had a triple identity bypass." Only by acting on these three would Australia establish its identity and forge its future.

Four decades on, how did Donald Horne assess Australia's progress towards these three national goals? I asked him this in two phone interviews in March and April 2005, the last of which turned out to be the final interview of his life. As he spoke, Horne apologised repeatedly for his wavering voice and what he said was his "wandering mind". He need not have worried: his thoughts were as cogent and incisive as ever.

On the country's status as a republic, a test which Australia has spectacularly failed to pass, Horne was surprisingly sanguine:

> I talked about the republic idea as a way to develop a sense of Australian awareness, which at the time I wrote The Lucky Country might be described as questions of national and cultural identity.
>
> Cultural identity is coming along quite well, I think. Menzies used to go around pretending to be British. People now don't quite understand that old Menzian thinking – it's simply gone.

Horne was well versed in this syndrome. After an early phase at Sydney University as a self-proclaimed anarchist, he travelled to Britain with his English wife, became a monarchist and even aspired to become a Conservative MP until Sir Frank Packer's offer of an editorship of a Sydney magazine snapped him out of it. And, according to him, the whole country snapped out of it: "Walking around the streets of Australia today and talking to people, assumptions are very different," he said. Still, he wanted to see more: the formal achievement of a republic:

> What's needed now is not more poetry – defining Australia in terms of the bush and eucalypts and so on; we need to define ourselves away from the bush myth. What we need is a constitution.
>
> There was all that claptrap about a head of state – and that's my fault – but being a republic would mean having a constitution something like Sweden's, which says that all power comes through the people in elections and referenda. So whenever you see the head of state, whoever it is, that person represents an idea, so you have a civic definition of Australia.
>
> I still remember with horror our bicentennial celebrations, in which we had not one politician able to make a speech about how Australia was the first country to define itself with a vote – it voted itself into Federation. Instead, they all wanted to talk about Anzac and the bush.

On the second task that Horne prescribed for the nation – involvement with Asia – he seemed to be quite pleased with the work of the past forty years. "By the end of the 1940s and early 1950s, Australia was already becoming engaged with Asia. A great reformer was Percy Spender, and he was advised by people half a generation ahead of me." Spender, the author of the Colombo Plan as well as the ANZUS Treaty while he was minister for external affairs under Menzies, once remarked that "no nation can escape its geography."

By 1990, Australia's trade was so heavily concentrated in Asia that it was, in economic terms, more Asian than most of the countries of Asia themselves. Horne continued: "Where we have failed is that our political class hasn't always been that hot at turning it into people's imaginations, although they are getting onto it now."

He gave all prime ministers from Harold Holt onwards some credit for advancing the Australian involvement with Asia. It may surprise Labor partisans that he acknowledged John Howard's contribution to the great project of Asian engagement. "Even John Howard has played a part, though sometimes lapsing." Horne said Howard's mimicry of George W. Bush's doctrine of the pre-emptive strike was a "muck-up – it's held things up and it's been a bloody pest." But, he said, Howard's personal diplomacy in Asia, which has been energetic and sustained, meant that "if he keeps going, Howard will probably be remembered as a man looking to Asia."

It was on the third proposal for Australia's future – technological and economic rejuvenation – that Horne seemed to think the country had made the greatest progress. He agreed that the economic reform program introduced by the Hawke–Keating government from 1983 was a threshold moment for Australia and that it was the reason why our slide down the ranking of wealthy countries had been arrested, and then reversed.

In *The Lucky Country*, Horne had written that renewal would surely require a dramatic change in the style of political leadership, and he didn't think that was terribly likely. It was 1964, and Menzies' long reign still had nearly two more years to run.

> Among those who are frightened by this perpetual state of Stand Easy – and it is an emotion breaking through political party loyalties – there is a feeling of distrust for their own nation; a fear that clever, responsible people will just not be found; that there will be no breakthrough of new men; things will just go on; no one will do the job. This sense of hopelessness may prove to be an accurate forecast.

For nearly twenty years it was. The Coalition prime ministers who succeeded Menzies were men of the status quo. When the conservatives' 23-year monopoly of federal power finally ended in 1972, Labor's leader was certainly a breakthrough man. But while Gough Whitlam turned out to be clever, he was not responsible enough for the times. Fiscally frightening, a visionary who launched Medicare and free universities but ran the Commonwealth into debt to pay for them, and not in power for long enough to make a lasting economic renovation, Whitlam was replaced by Malcolm Fraser, who immediately threw himself into doing nothing, economically speaking.

Finally, it was Bob Hawke and Paul Keating who broke through as the "new men", clever and responsible, who did away with the "perpetual state of Stand Easy" and changed Australia's national economic trajectory. Theirs was a winning good-cop-bad-cop partnership for nearly a decade – the popular knockabout prime minister, Hawke, winning elections while the stern and unrelenting treasurer, Keating, reformed the economy.

When Hawke's first minister for industry, John Button, took the job and looked around at his new constituency, he declared that Australian manufacturing was not an industry but an "industrial museum". The economy was highly protected behind soaring tariff walls. That made it deeply uncompetitive. There was a pervasive sense of entitlement and only a feeble impulse to compete. And this was perfectly logical. Why compete if you are protected? Why work hard to make a profit when you can coast? Why try to match the best in the world when you can make a comfortable living selling second-rate goods to a captive market?

The tariff walls put foreign goods at such a disadvantage that the laziest and most cobwebbed of Australian firms could survive comfortably. Likewise, rigid controls cosseted the banking and financial sectors from foreign competition. And a fixed exchange rate completed the defences against the world.

There were three principal losers from this system. First was the Australian consumer, who paid top-shelf prices for bottom-shelf merchandise.

Next were the competitive Australian industries of mining and farming. These sectors could thrive in open global competition but had to buy their machinery and borrow their money from companies and banks that were hopelessly inefficient and overpriced. They were world-class athletes running in the economic Olympics shackled to the iron ball of uncompetitive local suppliers. The income earners were in thrall to the rent-seekers.

Third was the national economy. A protected economy is an uncompetitive economy. In a protected system the "creative destruction" of a market economy, as Joseph Schumpeter described it, cannot function. If a system is designed to prop up every existing factory and job, then there is no capital or labour free to move into new areas of promise. The economic organisation is rigid when it should be fluid, static when it should be dynamic.

What Button saw was a chronically under-performing economy with sclerotic growth, high unemployment and a steadily declining relative national income. Another Hawke minister, John Dawkins, pointed out that Australia had "first-world living standards with a third-world industrial structure". It was a mismatch that could not continue. The relative price of what Australia sold to the world was in long-term decline, while the relative price of what Australia bought from the world was on a long-run rise.

Keating stripped away the comforting but ruinous protection of high tariffs, the tightly controlled financial system and the rigid, inflationary wages structure. He unceremoniously ended a century of protection, and forced Australia to compete in the world.

At the time, this historic transformation won him few friends. He insisted Australians abandon their failing economy before they understood the need. The wrenching change was absolutely essential and thoroughly unpopular. Even Donald Horne, the prophet, didn't recognise the messiah when he finally appeared. As late as 1998, Horne hadn't comprehended that the Hawke–Keating reform program was delivering the national economic salvation for which he had hoped. "The reform was concerned mainly with undoing some of the old controls and supports, not with thinking about the conditions of producing something new," he wrote.

Horne was not alone. The unofficial president of the Paul Keating fan club, the columnist and ABC broadcaster Phillip Adams, was a trenchant critic of Keating's reform program at the time that Keating was imposing it. Most on the left of Australian politics did not see the benefits of the reforms because they thought that economic progress must involve a bigger role for the state. But Keating saw that the country needed a thriving and energetic private sector, and the role of the state was already so big that it choked the competitive spirit. It fell to Keating to liberate it. He told me in a 2005 interview that, at the loneliest phase, he had the entire country ranged against him with only the Federal Parliamentary Press Gallery in support.

Today even John Howard, never a member of the Paul Keating fan club, nonetheless gives the Hawke–Keating government its due. George Megalogenis in his book *The Longest Decade* reports Howard as saying: "The two big things they did, really big things, in my judgment, were, obviously, financial deregulation and tariff reform. I thought tariff reform was their most courageous thing, given their constituency." Howard cannot resist taking some share of the credit himself: "But bear in mind, those reforms had our support." Which is true – the Coalition did not seek to block the reforms from its position on the Opposition benches. The reforms had bipartisan support. But it is also true that while the conservatives may have had the sense to acquiesce in fundamental reform, they had shown in twenty-three years in power that they did not have the courage to propose it.

Keating said:

> When one undertakes … such a broad set of fundamental changes, you know, you virtually upset at some stage or another every sector: the labour market, the manufacturers, the car makers, the textile makers, the footwear makers, you know, the states, the electricity companies. I mean, not that one has a check-list, but you do get around to offending everybody.
>
> But somebody has to give the country a break.

Not necessarily. Look at the world's other developed countries and you see that it is a very rare thing for a country to break out of complacency and inflict upon itself the pain necessary to bring about thoroughgoing economic revitalisation. That's the story of Japan for the last twenty years and of the countries of Western Europe for the last forty.

One of Europe's leading economic thinkers, Andre Sapir, visited Australia a couple of years ago and wanted to know how the country had managed to turn around its economic performance. He was told of the single-mindedness with which Keating pursued the task. He was told how sometimes the rest of the government lost its nerve, but Keating would never relent. He was told how the Treasurer had sometimes to stare down his Prime Minister to get his way. After hearing all this, Professor Sapir announced, with feeling: "In Europe, this is impossible!"

Australia's per capita income has now risen in the world ranking from fifteenth to eighth. In the last decade unemployment has halved; the country's unemployment rate is its lowest in thirty years. Net household wealth has doubled. Real wealth has increased by much more in the last fifteen years than in the previous thirty. In its 2006 assessment of this country, the Organisation for Economic Co-operation and Development reported that, "In the last decade of the twentieth century, Australia became a model for other OECD countries."

Australia, brags Peter Costello, has become not the poor white trash but "the strongman of Asia". If any Australian politician had advanced this claim at any time in the preceding thirty years, he or she would have been a laughing stock. Nobody laughs now.

The first time that anyone noticed that anything had really changed in Australia was in 1997. The economies of our main trading partners fell into deep crisis, and Australia was sure to follow. But, confounding all expectations, the country continued to boom.

For the Treasurer, Peter Costello, the new recognition of Australia's performance was crystallised in the comment of a leading Japanese policy maker. Costello gave the background to the comment:

> When I went to my first APEC finance ministers' meeting in Kyoto in 1996, it was the heyday of the Asian tigers and there was an unmistakable feeling that Australia was a country that was past it – we were tolerated, but barely. We were on the decline, in the presence of Asian tigers on the incline.

A year later, with Thailand, South Korea and Indonesia in various stages of international insolvency and Japan mired in its seventh year of recession, Costello turned up for the next APEC finance ministers' meeting to find the group being lectured by the then US treasury secretary, Larry Summers. Recalled Costello: "Larry Summers was bemoaning the fact that the US was carrying world growth and he said to this meeting, 'The world economy can't fly on one engine.'"

The top Japanese official in the room, Dr Eisuke Sakakibara, known in world financial markets as Mr Yen, shot back: "The world is not flying on one engine – there is also the Australian economy."

Costello: "The thing is, it was only half in jest – that's the point of the story. We came out as the strongman of Asia." Indeed, Australia became one of only two countries in the world to supply emergency liquidity to all the nations caught in the crisis. The other was Japan, the world's second biggest economy.

It was this island of Australian resilience in a sea of Asian turmoil and recession that moved the US economist Paul Krugman to write in *Fortune* magazine in 1998: "Australia, in case you didn't know, is the miracle economy of the world financial crisis." And five years later the length and strength of the Australian boom remained its distinguishing feature. "To a visitor from the northern hemisphere, Australia is like another planet," marvelled the *Economist* magazine in March 2003. "Even as the economies of America, Europe and Japan appear to be stumbling for the second time in less than three years, Australia continues to boom."

Most economists see no early end to the expansion. "We are in a twenty-year upswing," says John Edwards, HSBC Australia's chief economist. Edwards, one-time economic adviser to Paul Keating, in a paper for the Lowy Institute, writes of the novelty of this in the Australian experience:

> Two hundred years after Captain Phillip and the First Fleet arrived in Sydney Cove, Australians were accustomed to drought, flood and fire, to booms and busts. They had tried many economic theories, from penal serfdom, state government socialism, and protectionism, to free trade, uncaring capitalism, and dizzy speculation – sometimes apart, sometimes together. They had seen success and failure. They had experienced every circumstance except the one economic circumstance they most wanted and now least expected: a very long period in which everything simply got better and better.

It arrived in 1991. It continues.

And while the OECD holds Australia up as a model for successful economic reform, the country has also emerged as an exemplar in another sense. Unheralded and almost unnoticed, Australia has developed as a distinctive, and distinctively successful, socio-economic model. In this, it offers an alternative to the two familiar options of the American versus the European.

Australia is the only developed country that enjoyed faster economic growth than the US over the past decade. Yet it also offers universal healthcare and other social welfare benefits that the US does not. Unemployment is similar to America's, but without the glaring income disparities that characterise US growth.

It is a country that seems to have achieved a sweet spot, combining the vigour of American capitalism with the humanity of European welfare, yet suffering the drawbacks of neither. And it manages this while keeping a consistent budget surplus.

The US may be a rich country, but its bounty is very unevenly shared. The disparity in income, which has been widening for thirty years, has become so glaring that even the country's chief central banker has raised it as a concern. Central bankers are not known for their warm-heartedness, and the Federal Reserve chairman, Ben Bernanke, did not raise it as a matter of compassion or morality but as a threat to the national economic future. Widening inequality could make Americans "less willing to accept the dynamism … so essential to economic progress", he said in February of this year. In the last quarter-century, the top fifth of US income earners saw their average after-tax incomes rise by 69 per cent in real terms. The middle fifth enjoyed a 21 per cent increase. And the bottom fifth saw an increase of only 6 per cent, according to the Congressional Budget Office. So the difference in the rate of income gains between top and bottom is more than tenfold, 6 per cent against 69 per cent.

It will come as a surprise to many Australians, who are accustomed to hearing that income disparities have widened here in recent years, to learn that incomes across the spectrum have risen at a rather even rate. The Australian Bureau of Statistics reports that, over almost a decade, from 1994 to 2003, the average income of the top income group in Australia rose by 16 per cent, the middle by 14 per cent and the bottom by 12 per cent. The difference in the rate of income gain between the top and bottom is only one-third, 12 per cent against 16. Are there rich and poor? Naturally. Do the rich have vastly more than the poor? Of course. But the point is that all income groups in Australia have gained, at a surprisingly similar rate, from the boom of the last decade.

For the broad mass of its citizens, America has the health indicators of a much poorer country. Australia has chosen a more egalitarian policy set. Life expectancy is the fifth highest in the world. Child poverty is half the American rate. The US Institute of Medicine has estimated that 18,000 Americans die prematurely and unnecessarily each year because of lack of health insurance. That's six times the number who died in the 9/11 terrorist attacks. No one in Australia dies because of lack of health insurance.

But neither does Australia suffer the customary handicap that goes with a humane welfare system – a crushing burden of government spending. As a proportion of gross domestic product, total government spending in Australia is the third lowest in the OECD, and slightly less than in the US. The federal government has run a surplus in nine of the past ten years. Last year it paid off all outstanding federal debt – the federal government is debt-free for the first time since the 1970s.

John Howard is conscious that Australia has marked out its own place in between the American and European models:

> There is much in American society that I admire but I have long held the view that the absence of an effective safety net in that country means that too many needy citizens fall by the wayside. That is not the path that Australia will tread. Nor do we want the burdens of nanny-state paternalism that now weigh down many economies in Europe.

*

The Australian boom, now rolling into its seventeenth year, has been of incalculable advantage to John Howard. It is the merest commonsense that a people enjoying unprecedented prosperity, reasonably equally shared, will be inclined to perpetuate this condition. Insofar as they think the incumbent government is responsible, they will be inclined to re-elect it. As the former US president Woodrow Wilson said in 1912: "Prosperity is necessarily the first theme of a political campaign."

Howard has taken full credit, naturally. And he knows that the boom has been his greatest political ally. In an uncharacteristic moment of frankness, perhaps because he was addressing a gathering of conservative politicians from around the world, he said in 2002, "Clearly economic competence and the strength of a nation's economy is an enormous weapon in the hands of an incumbent government." It's telling that he should call it a "weapon" – not an asset to employ or an advantage to use, not a tool of work or a comfort for reassurance, but a weapon for inflicting harm.

If commonsense, Woodrow Wilson and John Howard are not enough to make the point that a strong economy works in favour of an incumbent government, we also have the work of the economics profession. Extensive research suggests that key economic indicators can be a better predictor of election outcomes than opinion polls. In particular, movements in the unemployment rate carry predictive power. Examining elections from 1966, Jackman and Marks found that for every one percentage point fall in the unemployment rate, an incumbent government can expect to be rewarded with a swing in its favour of 0.75 per cent in its share of the two-party preferred vote. Cameron and Crosby found the same relationship, but with a slightly smaller effect.

Australia's unemployment rate is still falling in early 2007. It was 5.3 per cent at the time of the 2004 election. In early 2007 it is 4.5 per cent. Based on the economists' modelling, the Howard government could expect a swing in its favour of about another half of a percentage point in its share of the vote, based on the current unemployment rate.

And there is a deeper political effect than this mechanically observed one. Consider the transformative effect that the boom has had on Australian society. John Edwards writes:

> It proved to be an economic expansion so sustained, so deep and widespread in its impact, so novel in its characteristics, that the lives of Australians, their hopes and plans, their work and leisure, their wealth and incomes, their politics, the way they saw themselves and their country and the ways it related to other countries, even the way they thought about their past, began to be changed by it. The most remarkable change, however, is an elusive but discernible increase in Australians' confidence in their future.

Howard is very much alive to the effects of wealth on Australian attitudes. As he put it in an interview with me in 2004:

The old story ... you see a bloke driving by in a Rolls-Royce in America, you say, "I'll have one of those one day." But sometimes the old Australian [attitude] resents the fact that somebody else has got it.

Now, I think that's changing. I think that's changing quite a lot with younger people. Younger people now are more aspirational. There's a very important change that's come over our society. Young people now are very disdainful of trade unions. They think they belong to a bygone era.

Howard sees that younger Australians perceive great prosperity not as a condition that's impossibly remote, but as something that's available to them. It's not something to get resentful about, it's something to get busy with. The political meaning of this confidence and aspirationalism is that it creates a whole new generation of Liberal voters.

Can Howard take credit for Australia's boom? He cannot take credit for the Hawke–Keating reforms, but he is responsible for decisions since 1996.

The early reform record of the Howard–Costello government is the subject of near-universal praise among the economics profession. One early decision was to ensure the Reserve Bank was independent of government in deciding whether to raise or drop interest rates. This helped the Reserve Bank under Ian Macfarlane to produce the best monetary management in the world. Another was the commitment to keep the national Budget in balance or in surplus. A third decision was to improve budget transparency, with Treasury required to release publicly a mid-year review of progress in achieving budget outcomes and a snapshot of the latest economic activity. Other significant changes were the reform of the tax system, introducing the GST, and, more recently, creating a single national industrial relations system based on individual contracts. In last year's Budget, Costello announced dramatic reform of superannuation to improve savings, which will not only help retirees but should also add to national savings. And the conspicuous reform of Howard's fourth term is the introduction of WorkChoices. This is a deregulation of the workplace that is designed to increase flexibility for employers. In the event of a recession, it will probably allow employers to cut the cost of their work-forces by reducing wages and conditions.

As Howard and Costello's term in office has lengthened, it is clear that the government's reform drive has faltered. It has failed to manage prop-erly the problems of success. Productivity growth has slowed. After such a long boom there is a shortage of skilled workers and the country suffers from under-investment in new infrastructure. With the economy approaching full capacity, the former Reserve Bank governor Ian Macfar-lane announced in 2005 that the rate of potential economic growth had slowed: "We should get used to GDP growth with a two or a three in front of the decimal point, rather than a three or a four as we had become accustomed to throughout most of the expansion." Further, Australia has a chronic current account deficit of a yawning 6 per cent of GDP.

On these grounds, a growing chorus of economists now argues that the Howard government is missing a once-in-a-generation opportunity to make more, necessary reforms. The ANZ Bank's chief economist, Saul Eslake, complimented Costello on his early reforms, but judged that "the fact that the government has not undertaken real reform of the tax system would have to rank as one of the greatest missed opportunities in the last fifty years." Eslake made this point:

> The commodities boom has created windfall gains for the Com-monwealth revenue, if you include the Budget to be announced next week [May 2006], of upwards of $100 billion spread over the last four budgets. But the government hasn't saved any of these ... gains. I struggle to think of anything they've done in recent years to strengthen the resilience of the economy for when the commod-ities boom ends, to increase productivity, or to enable fundamental reform.

A Macquarie Bank economist, Rory Robertson, quipped that "the economy has done more for the government than the government has done for the economy."

What does the Treasurer say to this criticism? Asked to respond in an interview in his office last year, Costello leaned back in his chair, flung his arms towards the ceiling, and boomed:

> This idea that there's a once-for-all magical fix – done that. I did the biggest tax reform in Australian history in 2000, but they're all back on it again! Now, you could do the next biggest now and they'd all be on it again in four years' time.

It was the voice of a man pleased with his record, happy with his creation. It lent some credence to Paul Keating's assessment of Costello as "a complacent, business-as-usual treasurer".

Complacency was a terrible provocation to Donald Horne. It seemed to him that the minerals boom of the last few years risked reinstating the national complacency: "It's quite appalling to discover people saying today that Australia is still the lucky country because we have all these minerals," Horne said in his final interview. "There's still a bloody lucky country mentality!"

Contrary to general belief, the big take-off in commodities prices is a tailwind assisting Australia only slightly, and only in the last four years. It is certainly having a powerful effect in the areas that directly service the mining industry. House prices in Perth are bounding ahead with rises of 30 per cent a year, for instance. But its overall effect on the national economy is marginal. The up-tick in mining output in 2005 contributed a mere 0.1 of a percentage point to the national economic growth of 2.7 per cent.

But no matter how much, or how little, credit Howard can take for Australia's long boom, Labor has allowed itself to be put into a position where it can take none at all. This is the most profound mistake of political strategy that the Labor Party has made in its eleven years on the Opposition benches.

Neither Paul Keating nor Bob Hawke has ever received the credit they deserve for saving Australia from its long, slow slide into economic hopelessness. Partly it's because of the long lag between the pain of the reforms and the gain of the prosperity they generated – it was almost a decade between the advent of the first Hawke–Keating government in 1983 and the dawning of the great boom in 1991. And partly it's because the remarkable nation-changing accomplishment of economic turnaround was obscured by everything else that intruded – Keating's messy political assassination of Hawke to seize the throne, the 1990 "recession we had to have", and the personal unpopularity of Keating with the electorate.

It was because of this – Keating's unpopularity – that the party was so reluctant to have anything to do with him. This continued even into the last federal election. Amid the razzle-dazzle of the Labor campaign launch in Brisbane, former leaders were feted, and Mark Latham ostentatiously hugged Gough Whitlam. Paul Keating, though, was treated like a disgraced relative one was obliged to invite but was ashamed to embrace. He was brought in through a side door and edited out of Labor's broadcast TV footage. It was the nadir of his exile.

This repudiation, Labor realised after the devastating result at the polls, was a mistake. The party lost the last election in large part because voters decided Latham and Labor could not be trusted to run the economy. The party had done so much of the work of rebuilding the economy, yet had no credibility on economic policy.

Keating did not enjoy his exile, but he thinks Labor suffered more than he did. "Fundamentally, the Labor Party never believed in the model," he said to me in 2005. By "the model", he meant an open, modern, market-based economy, the economy that John Howard and Peter Costello inherited from Labor, but a concept that Labor itself, post-Hawke and post-Keating, let slip. Keating continued:

> The whole Hawke–Keating model for Australia didn't have to happen. The unlikely thing is it came from a Labor government. Labor

governments and Labor parties mostly believed in big budget deficits, they believed in higher tariffs and managed exchange rates and controlled financial markets. The Labor Party never believed in the model that Hawke and I gave the country, but it happened. The country got a very great break from it.

But Labor failed to get the break. Hawke and Keating had been concerned with how to create wealth, but after 1996 Labor returned to its historical preoccupation, not with how to create wealth, but with how to redistribute it. By discarding the economic model, by rejecting the builders and their handiwork, Labor also threw away the voter base it brought with it, according to Keating:

> It's a fundamentally flawed strategy. The Labor Party has given up the middle-class, middle-ground, sole-employer, self-employed, small-business voter that Bob Hawke and I generated for it. That's why Kim Beazley got a majority of votes in 1998 but not a majority of seats – because he couldn't get the distribution [of votes in the seats where they were needed to win government] because the Labor Party had already run away from our record …
>
> There's a decade lost and the brand fades. People don't tie up the policies with the outcome. A decade of prosperity is a structural benefit for the Liberal Party even though the Liberal Party didn't create it in the first place. And of course every time the Labor Party tried to win in 1998, 2001 and the last election, 2004, the further it got away from the internationalising model of the Labor government, 1983–96, the less well it did.

After the gut-punch of the 2004 result, Labor realised its error. It decided to rehabilitate Keating. "We have decided to bring him in from the cold," Kim Beazley told me in August 2006. In doing this, Labor decided to confront the problem of its credibility on economic policy. Since the 2004 election, it has recognised the economy as the central political battleground. It has acknowledged the country is in a rare period of extended prosperity. And after being airbrushed out of Labor family photos for almost a decade, Uncle Paul is now back in the frame. Kim Beazley – before his departure – and his finance frontbenchers, Wayne Swan and Stephen Smith, three of the men who had earlier sought to hold Keating at arm's length, began publicly to acknowledge his legacy.

Kevin Rudd has continued to try to recover Labor's standing. In a speech to the Business Council of Australia in January, he contrasted Howard's economic performance with Keating's: "If Australia now had the same terms of trade as we did when Paul Keating was in office, the current account deficit would be 10 per cent of GDP – enough to put us on constant watch from the IMF." And he dismissed the government's claim of fiscal responsibility: "Riding the tax windfall from a resources boom to budget surplus, is easy, not tough."

For the preceding decade, Labor had been particularly spooked by the peak 17 per cent mortgage rate that banks charged during the Keating era. The government used this to crushing effect against the ALP; indeed, it used it so relentlessly that it became reflexive. It was the stock response to any Labor complaint about government economic policy. I call it the government's Spinal Tap defence.

In the cult movie This Is Spinal Tap, a spoof documentary on the life of a failing heavy metal band, the group's guitarist takes us on a tour of his collection of prized musical instruments. After showing off his favourite electric guitar – the one with the flame painted on it – the long-haired, gum-chewing Cockney Nigel Tufnel brings us to his favourite amplifier. "It's very, very special because if you can see" – drawing attention to the calibrations on the knobs on the face of the amplifier – "the numbers all go to eleven." A normal volume knob is marked from zero to ten, but Nigel's favourite goes up to eleven.

The reporter wants to know if this unique calibration makes the amplifier louder.

NIGEL (triumphantly): Well, it's one louder, isn't it? It's not ten. You see, most blokes, you know, will be playing at ten. What we do is if we need that extra push over the cliff ... you know what we do?

REPORTER: Put it up to eleven.

NIGEL: Eleven. Exactly. One louder.

REPORTER: Why don't you just make ten louder and make ten be the top number, and make that a little louder?

NIGEL (looking blank, chews his gum for a long moment before replying defiantly): These go to eleven.

No matter what Labor said in attacking his record on interest rates, Howard replied that, under Labor, interest rates went to 17 per cent. Even after Howard misled the electorate in the 2004 campaign with his promise to "keep interest rates at record lows" – misleading because the Reserve Bank, not the government, sets interest rates – he kept up the Spinal Tap defence. "Yours went to seventeen." Even after the Reserve Bank raised rates three times, exposing Howard's election promise as the falsehood it had always been, he kept it up. In Question Time, he called the peak mortgage rate under Labor in 1989 "the notorious 17 per cent", "the dizzy heights of 17 per cent" and "the bitterly remembered heights of 17 per cent". Say what you like, Howard said with a dogged imperturbability of which Nigel would be proud, but yours went to seventeen.

Finally, in parliament in August 2006, Labor's treasury spokesman, Wayne Swan, reminded Howard that interest rates had hit 21 per cent in 1982 under the then Liberal treasurer, John Howard. Incredibly, it was the first time that the Opposition had used this on Howard. It seemed to disarm him. He lost his Spinal Tap defence.

It had taken Labor a decade to do this, a decade to point out that Howard's rate peak was four percentage points higher than Keating's. Why now? Beazley said: "We have been waiting for this for a long time – it's finally reached the point where interest rates repayments on mortgages are more burdensome than in 1989." The Reserve Bank had just raised official rates for the third time since Howard's low-interest election.

How could it be that, with the average mortgage rate today at about 7.8 per cent, repayments are higher than under the notorious 17 per cent? It is because today's buyers struggle with such huge mortgages that even though interest rates are much lower, the proportion of their income that goes towards servicing them is larger. As Labor crowed, it took an average 7 per cent of household incomes to meet mortgage interest repayments in the Hawke–Keating years, but since the last election the figure has hit 7.9 per cent.

It took Labor a full decade to realise that, in abandoning Keating because of his unpopularity, it had also surrendered its claim to Keating's historic importance and to the prosperity he had bequeathed Australia.

Wayne Swan said in 2006 that Labor has "deliberately set out to take head-on the accusation that Keating's record was worse than the Coalition's". It is too late. The boom, in the electorate's mind, belongs to Howard. Asked which party is the better economic manager, Australians, by a margin of almost two to one, name the Howard government.

The Lucky Country decided to make its own luck. The political party that made the decisive break failed to take credit for its own accomplishments. Now it's too late. John Howard owns the national prosperity as a political asset or, in his own words, a "political weapon".

Alan Renouf, one of Australia's most experienced diplomats, was the secretary of the Department of Foreign Affairs until, as he puts it, "Malcolm Fraser kicked me out after that stuff-up in China." We have his kicking-out to thank for the book that he published in 1979, perhaps the toughest insider critique of Australian foreign policy ever written. Its title: *The Frightened Country.*

The writing of the book qualifies Renouf for a peculiar distinction. When he saw that the then prime minister was determined to force him out of his job as one of Canberra's most important mandarins – based on a false accusation of leaking official documents during a visit to China – Renouf arranged to leave the job to go to a new post as Australian Ambassador to Washington DC.

He took up the ambassador's post, and the elegant old ambassadorial residence that goes with it, not to cap a distinguished career managing Australia's most important alliance but to write his book. This must make it one of the most comfortable and well-funded writing sinecures in Australian publishing history. As soon as he finished the book, he resigned his post and retired to Australia. "I was the only ambassador to Washington to resign," he chuckles today.

His thesis was that an "unreasoning fearfulness" sits at the heart of Australia's relations with the world. We live in fear of our neighbourhood. That fear has several deep consequences for the way Australia conducts itself.

He pointed out that Australia has a remarkably short history of making its own decisions in foreign policy. When the states, British colonies all, federated in 1901 to form Australia, Britain continued to make Australian foreign policy. We did not even bother to have our own representatives abroad. Canberra appointed its first ambassador in 1939 when the government decided that Australia needed its own voice in Washington.

Renouf wrote:

> Like a child, Australia has shown a marked inclination to "stay with
> mother", first Britain and then the US, or, as Bruce Grant has felic-
> itously put it, to be the "spear carrier to the chief".
>
> One of the most persistent aggravations during my career as an
> Australian diplomat has been the reluctance by most Australian
> governments to formulate and execute a foreign policy designed to
> promote the distinctive Australian interest. The governing and lazy
> approach has nearly always been to ascertain what Britain, and later
> the US, thought and follow that.
>
> If Australia's two great friends disagreed – as they did in the 1956
> Suez War – Australian diplomacy floundered. This is a remarkable
> contrast to what might have been expected from a young and
> wealthy country.

Of whom were we afraid? Renouf argued that we have always been
afraid of someone. He ticked off the list of former enemies, real or perceived. In the nineteenth century it was the Russians, as the fortifications
at La Pérouse and Fort Denison in Sydney attest. And there was even a
moment when some American whaling ships that turned up in Sydney
Harbour were thought to have designs on the colony.

The Russians made a reprise as the enemy during the Cold War. And
though they were a real enemy, they were not as big an enemy as Australia's conservative governments claimed. In 1979 Renouf wrote:

> The current source of fear is the USSR. Why should Australia be
> frightened? Any such view as Defence Minister Jim Killen [in the
> Fraser Cabinet] once expressed – that the Soviet presence in the
> Indian Ocean is a threat to Australia's security – does not makes
> sense. Why would the USSR want to threaten Australia? To conceive
> the average small Soviet presence in the Indian Ocean as even
> remotely threatening to Australia is a fantasy. Should a real Soviet

threat to Australia develop, it could only happen as one among many circumstances inevitably engaging the attention of the US and other Western countries. Fear of the USSR is irrational and out of date. The USSR's conduct calls for vigilance, not fear.

Then there was, of course, the fear of Asian hordes, a long-running terror in the Australian imagination. The origin of this fear was the influx of the Asians, chiefly Chinese, who came to work and invest in Australia in the nineteenth century. In response, the White Australia Policy was instituted, which defined Australian immigration and identity for a century. It was the social analogue to the economic policy of protectionism, the belief that Australia was best served by walling itself off from the world.

The pressures that led to White Australia started to build almost as soon as Edward Hargraves found his "grain of gold" in a waterhole near Bathurst in 1851, galvanising the great Australian gold rushes. The national population when Hargraves reported his find was 430,000. In the next twenty years, the fortune seekers to descend on Australia multiplied the population to a total of 1.7 million, a quadrupling in a single generation.

Among the inrush were Chinese miners and traders and shopkeepers and coolies and investors. They numbered a scant 40,721. As a share of the total Australian population, the Chinese proportion peaked at just 3.3 per cent, in 1861. But they were conspicuous because they were the biggest non-white group and their appearance and customs marked them out as alien. That alone might have been enough. But there was also an economic resentment. The Chinese miners were competition for gold, and, after the gold rushes, as the economy turned down, they were resented as competitors for jobs.

According to an editorial in the *Sydney Morning Herald* in that year, the behaviour of the Chinese in Australian society was a model:

> They are not seen rolling about the street in a state of drunkenness; they are not covered with rags. They do not cast their poor upon the

public charity. They have a very extensive organisation to relieve and protect each other.

And big Chinese investors set up some of Australia's most important industries, including the important Queensland crops of sugar and bananas, financed with Chinese money and worked by Chinese labour, as Henry Reynolds recorded in *North of Capricorn*.

In New South Wales in that same year, out of a total population of 350,860, the Chinese numbered only 12,988, or just 3.7 per cent. But this, it so happened, was an intolerable number to the white population. One of the major petitions to the NSW government that year complained that:

> Their idolatrous customs, moral depravity, and detestable habits, are viewed with a constantly increasing disgust and dislike by all classes ... Your petitioners as loyal British citizens, cannot appreciate the extension of any of their peculiar rights and privileges to the Chinese; who, being aliens in blood, morals, country and religion, are presumed to have no legitimate claims.

The bitterness about the Chinese came to a political head in 1888, which Eric Rolls, in his excellent book on the Chinese in Australia, *Sojourners*, describes as "the most dubious year in our development". The events of that year, wrote Rolls, "finally lifted us clean out of Asia where geography placed us and laid us down again in the same position as an awkward slab of Europe".

With the economy slowing dramatically and popular indignation at its peak, the decision to impose White Australia was crystallised by a newspaper ad. A new rush was beginning, not for gold but for rubies. A prospector had bent down and plucked from the sandy bed of the Hale River near Alice Springs a handful of the stones. When assayed in London, they were pronounced to be the equal of the finest Siam rubies, worth ten times the price of diamonds. A whole new frenzy began.

One adventurer placed an advertisement in the *Northern Territory Times* seeking an experienced bushman to lead a party of 500 Chinese to prospect for rubies in the MacDonnell Ranges. That was all it took. Rallies and marches and petitions and, decisively, political pressure from the trade unions moved the governments of the colonies to impose strict new bans on Chinese arrivals. They were led by Henry Parkes, premier of New South Wales and the man rightly remembered as the Father of Federation. The colourful and charismatic former journalist was also the father of White Australia.

And the rubies? As Australian gems started to flood the world market, a new appraisal in London discovered that they had too low a percentage of crystalline alumina, specifically 23.44 per cent against the 90 per cent of the best Asian rubies. They weren't rubies at all but garnets. The rush ended as abruptly as it had begun.

Of the 40,721 Chinese who had come to Australia, 36,049 eventually left. This was Australia's experience of the so-called Asian hordes. It was a defining moment for the country's social and political evolution. The Chinese, never many in number, lingered in the collective national consciousness as the alien masses for which Australia has spent the rest of its history anxiously scanning the horizon.

And, of course, half a century later, Asian hordes did indeed assemble on the horizon in the form of the Japanese Imperial Forces. The reality of the Japanese campaign to take Australia in the Second World War vindicated the many imaginary threats that had stalked the popular consciousness. So when the Japanese were pacified and the Asian threat vanished, the fear of Asia did not.

Sometimes it was supposed to be China that threatened Australia, at other times Indonesia, and often it was just an unarticulated and undefined suspicion that shadowy forces somewhere to our north were plotting against us. Witness the phenomenal success of John Marsden's 'Tomorrow' series of novels for young adults, the first of which, *Tomorrow When the War Began*, was published in 1993. The series sold 1.3 million copies, smashing all Australian sales records. The books tell the thrillingly terrifying story of a teenage girl's survival in the Australian bush when a foreign army invades and occupies the country. The enemy is never named. All we know is that it is from somewhere in Asia, and, piling the incredible upon the implausible, that New Zealand tries to help us.

Indonesia has often been pressed into the role of enemy when no more feasible threat existed. Today when the Australian army conducts ground manoeuvres, in the minds of the troops the notional enemy is Indonesia. Wrote Renouf in *The Frightened Country*: "Indonesia is of great strategic importance to Australia, astride the lines of communication directly north and indirectly west and east. If there is to be a threat to security in the foreseeable future, it could only come from Indonesia."

The menacing overtones are not entirely imaginary. The country was a communist sympathiser under its first president, Sukarno, and was close to the USSR in the early days of the Cold War. It has been the source of violent aggression against its neighbours four times in the past fifty years.

The first was when Indonesia in 1954 laid claim to sovereignty over the neighbouring territory of West New Guinea, which was a colony of the Netherlands. The Dutch refused the claim. Australia, wary of Indonesia's trustworthiness as a neighbour, supported the Dutch. When Indonesia did not get its way through diplomacy, it started covert troop deployments to take the territory by force. From 1960 it secretly sent armed infiltrators into the territory. It then signed an arms pact with the USSR, and in 1962 landed paratroopers in West New Guinea. The Netherlands yielded. West New Guinea is now the Indonesian province of Irian Jaya.

Next came the Konfrontasi, or Confrontation, crisis. The new Federation of Malaysia came into being in 1963, a voluntary union of Malaya, Singapore, Sarawak and North Borneo. Indonesia, which controlled most of the island of Borneo, decided that it would take the opportunity to try to wrest control of the balance of the island before it could be incorporated into the new federation. Sukarno ordered the Indonesian army to "crush" the new nation of Malaysia. Australia, together with Britain and New Zealand, deployed forces in support of the Malaysians.

The Australians and Indonesians looked at each other through the sights of their rifles and fought some skirmishes, and though there were no fatalities it was a deeply troubling episode. For a brief moment, there was a real prospect that Australia and Indonesia could be in a state of open warfare with each other. It was in the midst of this crisis that Menzies rushed through the contract to buy the F-111 bomber in 1963, explicitly to pose a threat to Indonesia, and implicitly to appear to be a tough and decisive leader in the forthcoming elections. Konfrontasi ended when Sukarno was overtaken by political strife at home.

Then Indonesia's next president, Soeharto, ordered the army to invade and annex East Timor in 1975. This was the source of much agonising inside the Australian government, and both Gough Whitlam and Malcolm Fraser warned Jakarta not to use force, yet Australia ultimately acquiesced in the Indonesian armed conquest of its tiny neighbour.

As with West New Guinea, so with East Timor. When push came to shove, Australia was not prepared to risk armed confrontation with Indonesia in order to protect a smaller neighbour from Jakarta's ambitions.

The fourth case of Indonesian aggression was less overt because Indonesia employed proxies rather than regulars, yet it still precipitated a major crisis. Soeharto's successor as president, Habibie, decided to relax Jakarta's grip on East Timor. He allowed the East Timorese the opportunity to vote for independence in 1999. When they seized it with both hands, the Indonesian army looked to exact a price for this act of rebelliousness. The army organised gangs of local thugs to wreak havoc in East Timor. In the face of murder and mayhem, the Australian public was incensed. The Howard government mobilised and led a UN mission to intervene and quash the Indonesian army–inspired violence. The mission, commanded by Peter Cosgrove, succeeded so spectacularly and with so little bloodshed that it became an international model for peacemaking missions.

So Indonesia has used force in the cause of territorial expansion in the past. This has twice prompted Australia to deploy its armed forces to frustrate Indonesian ambitions, once to protect Malaysia and once to protect East Timor. On two other occasions Australia has decided that it was more prudent to permit Indonesian adventurism to proceed, believing that it was wiser to tolerate Indonesia's appetite for gobbling up small neighbours than it was to try to deter aggression and enforce international norms of conduct in our region. Indonesia's official relations with Australia are often testy. The level of cultural affinity is zero. People-to-people contact is largely quarantined to the island of Bali, the equivalent of confining your people-to-people contact with the US to one of the islands of Hawaii, or with Japan to the island of Okinawa.

All this is enough to qualify Jakarta as a candidate for Australian uneasiness. Yet does it make it an actual threat to Australia? Or is it just a convenient bogeyman for an obsolete yet persistent Australian fear? Australia's forces have decisive advantage over Indonesia's in every realm – on land, at sea and in the air. Not only does Indonesia lack capability, it also lacks intent. Indonesia is a poor, weak country whose army has always been primarily concerned with looking inwards rather than outwards. It has been principally occupied with holding together a fragile and artificial amalgam of 220 million people drawn from 300 different ethnic groups speaking more than 700 languages, living on 6000 islands. For all but the last eight years of its existence, the army has been busy imposing the will of Indonesia's dictators on its people. It has never had territorial designs on Australia.

Still, you can see how it could be sketched as a frightening prospect. As a potential enemy, it's big enough to look intimidating, it's Muslim enough to seem alien, it's close enough to be worrying, and it's so poorly understood in Australia to be plausible as a threat. Gareth Evans, the former foreign minister, liked to say that there were no two neighbours anywhere in the world as different from each other as Australia and Indonesia.

*

Our national fearfulness explained for Renouf another of the central instincts of Australian foreign policy. He wrote:

> Australians have traditionally and somewhat irrationally been vaguely apprehensive that Asians will some day sweep down from the north to fill their enormous empty spaces; the obvious source is Indonesia. If this happened, Australia would need help. The only supplier of effective help would be the US.

Australia's exaggerated fear gave it an outsized need for reassurance, and it responded with a hungry embrace of a "great and powerful friend". It clung to Britain until the fiction of London's defence assurances to Australia was exposed by the Second World War, and then turned to the US.

"The US responded during the war in her own interests and Australians lulled themselves into the comforting conclusion that the US would do so again should the need arise," Renouf wrote. "The Australian governments assessed that the need was constantly close to arising." The ANZUS Treaty, signed in 1951 and taking effect in 1952 when fear of international communism was at a high point, formalised the Australian need for reassurance.

Foreign policy in the Howard government's third and fourth terms has been dominated by Howard's determination to be in the very front rank of the US's supporters in its most difficult undertaking, the invasion of Iraq. This is entirely consistent with, indeed was prefigured by, Renouf's analysis twenty-eight years ago. It was a feature of Coalition governments, he argued, to regard as an objective the best possible relationship with the US: "This end was so pursued that Australia gained a reputation in some countries as an American client state. This was seldom true but outsiders were given good reason to suspect it."

More than a quarter of a century later, what sort of Australia does Renouf look out on? What threats do we face? How have we come to regard the US alliance? Is it still the Frightened Country?

Renouf, now eighty-seven years old and in the midst of writing a series of lectures on the history of the British Empire, sets out his own sense of the risks, then gives a diagnosis of the collective Australian perception. In his own view, Australia is a country without much to worry about in defence terms:

> Now, there is virtually no enemy. The only country that people mention to me as a threat is Indonesia. But they don't have the capacity to invade. And even if they started now they would take fifteen years and we'd have plenty of warning.
>
> And despite John Howard's efforts to talk up the terrorist threat, there is little real threat to Australia. Of course, the terrorist threat to Australians overseas is real. But in Australia it is very limited. I think there's a large political element to this terrorist threat in Australia. And as for the "Asian hordes", I think that's probably finished and any reasonable person would realise that.

Yet that's not the way that the collective Australian mind perceives it.

> We see ourselves sitting in a continent of great wealth, with more every day, and we are sometimes the subject of envy of other countries. We are sitting here lonely at the end of the world. And everyone around us is very different.
>
> Australia is apprehensive about the world. It's not a fear of invasion by another country, it's that the world is unstable and we are not sure what will happen and we are not happy about that.
>
> In the last resort, we still need a protector, though we are uncertain of any threat and where it may come from. And we find it cosy to have the Americans as our great friend. The average Australian thinks that whenever we need the US, they will be there.

So, still fearful, we still comfort ourselves with the notion of a hotline: we can pick up and dial 000, confident that, at the other end, the phone will ring and be answered and an emergency force dispatched.

Renouf has a very different conception of the US alliance. "The ANZUS pact doesn't mean anything like the Australians think it does. Percy Spender wanted a NATO-style guarantee. It wasn't at all what he got." Spender, Menzies' foreign minister, pressed Washington for a treaty that replicated Article 5 of the North Atlantic Treaty – that an armed attack on one party to the treaty shall be deemed to be an armed attack on all. But the US refused. Instead, the ANZUS Treaty says that:

> Each Party recognises that an armed attack in the Pacific Area on any of the Parties would be dangerous to its own peace and safety and declares that it would act to meet the common danger in accordance with its constitutional processes.

Renouf points out that this is more vague and less compelling than the NATO pact, that there is no commitment to the use of armed force, and that the rider about "constitutional processes" brings to bear the constitutional struggle in the US between the Congress and the presidency about the president's power to make war.

How would this tension be resolved in the event that Australia were to call on Washington for help? What would the "constitutional processes" entail exactly? The US Ambassador to Australia, Robert McCallum, was asked this question during an appearance at the National Press Club in February 2006. He replied that he didn't know. Then he went on to volunteer cheerfully: "I've never read the treaty. I've never done the constitutional analysis and I would imagine that there would be a vast difference of opinions among academics and practising lawyers and politicians as to what might be required."

This was an extraordinary moment. The ANZUS Treaty is the structural mainstay of the alliance. And the alliance is the centrepiece of Australia's national security and diplomacy. The country has put tremendous store by it for half a century. Yet the treaty rests so lightly in the consciousness of the superpower that even its ambassador to Canberra had not troubled to read its 840 words. Neither does McCallum's description of the constitutional situation inspire any confidence in the value of the treaty. In the event that Australia might want the US to invoke it, and even if the US were interested in obliging, the ambassador painted a picture of utter confusion in Washington. His underlying message to Australia on the ANZUS Treaty: don't count on it.

Alan Renouf concurs. He continues:

> Even when the US Senate ratified it, John Foster Dulles [US ambassador at large and later secretary of state] told the Senate Foreign Affairs Committee not to worry about it. It doesn't oblige them to do anything.
>
> And when we have needed it, the US has never responded. During Confrontation. In East Timor.

It is true that when Australian forces faced the Indonesians during the Confrontation crisis in 1964, on the only occasion when Australia formally sought to invoke ANZUS, Washington refused. It's also true that when Howard first decided to mobilise an international coalition to restore peace in East Timor, the initial response from the Clinton Administration was a rebuff, including a rather insulting remark from Clinton's national security adviser, Sandy Berger, comparing Australia's problem to that of his daughter's messy apartment – not his responsibility. Eventually, the US did support Canberra politically and militarily, though it did not commit any ground forces. Yet Howard refers to ANZUS as Australia's "security guarantee", knowing that it is actually no guarantee at all. And on the day after the US Ambassador confessed his ignorance of the treaty, the Foreign Minister, Alexander Downer, referred to it in the House of Representatives as "our key security guarantee".

Alan Renouf is a critic of John Howard's approach to the US alliance. "John Howard is George Bush's greatest supporter in the world." Renouf was one of the forty-three former top officials to sign a well-publicised statement in 2004 opposing the invasion of Iraq. The former defence chiefs, diplomats and intelligence bosses said that the government had joined the invasion on the basis of the "deception of the Australian people", which was "wrong and dangerous". Kevin Rudd at the time called it "an unprecedented attack on the government of the day" over foreign policy.

Renouf sees, however, that Howard's approach to the US alliance is working for him politically. Despite all the problems, dangers and deceptions of the invasion of Iraq and so-called war on terror, "John Howard is coming out of it pretty well – let's face it."

Howard is a deft handler of the Frightened Country. He knows our fears and phobias and he is masterful in playing on them, deploying them, managing them, manoeuvring them. He does two things. He prods our fears. And then he offers us reassurance. He inflames and then soothes, supplies the anxiety and also the solution.

One of the leading defence intellectuals in the US, Joseph Nye, the head of the Kennedy School of Government at Harvard and a former senior official at the Pentagon during the Clinton Administration, has written that "Security is like oxygen – you tend not to notice it until you begin to lose it, but once that occurs there is nothing else that you will think about."

John Howard wants us to think about our oxygen. He knows that, ever since September 11, 2001, we fear terrorist attack. Sixty per cent of us have said we think that Australia is likely – or very likely – to be subject to international terrorist attack sometime in the next five years, according to a survey conducted in late 2002 and early 2003 by Anglicare.

The odds of death by terrorist attack are extremely low. Since 1900, a total of twenty-two people have died at the hands of terrorists in Australia. Outside Australia, 140 Australians have died in terrorism attacks in the same period. You are better advised statistically to spend your psychic energy worrying about diet and traffic risks than terrorism.

But it's not about risk. It's about how we feel about the risk. Some types of danger frighten us much more than others, regardless of the actual level of risk. In the same year in which about 3000 people died from terrorism in the US, 42,000 died in traffic accidents. Has America declared a War on Traffic Accidents? Of course not. Is this irrational? Yes, but we're human, and irrationality is wired into our brains.

Howard knows we're anxious about Indonesia. A Lowy Institute poll last year found that when Australians were asked whether they agreed on a scale of 1 to 10 with the proposition that "Australia was right to worry about Indonesia as a military threat," the average response was 6.2 – in other words, yes. Asked whether "Indonesia is a dangerous source of Islamic terrorism," the response averaged 6.5.

Curiously, Australians have been becoming increasingly frightened of Indonesia for thirty years. Polling by the ANU's Ian McAllister shows that thirty years ago, one in ten Australians ranked Indonesia as a security threat. In the early 1980s, the proportion reached 25 per cent. In the latest available data, from 2001, it had climbed to 31 per cent. How does this compare to our perceptions of the threat posed by other countries? Next came China, rated a threat by only 9 per cent of Australians. "What appears to have happened is that there's been a consistent and incremental increase in the proportion of people who've identified Indonesia as a short- to medium-term security threat to Australia," says McAllister. And that was before the Bali bombing.

The Prime Minister connects these fears and uses them, for example, to justify keeping Australian troops in Iraq. "The terrorists would use our withdrawal as a recruiting ground, particularly in Indonesia. Why does he [Labor leader Kim Beazley] want to give a propaganda boost to JI in Indonesia?" says Howard, JI meaning Jemaah Islamiyah. He has used this argument repeatedly – support my policy or there will be a proliferation of terrorists in Indonesia. Implicit is that these newly minted Indonesian terrorists would target Australians and Australia.

John Howard, who once famously articulated his vision for a "relaxed and comfortable" Australia, now has a new ideal for the nation. He wants, he said during the last election campaign, a "secure" Australia.

It seems perverse, then, that he spent the last campaign making us feel at risk. From the day he called the 2004 election, the Prime Minister told us to fear for our prosperity – a vote for Labor is a vote for higher interest rates. More subtly, he drew attention to the risks to our physical security. He accused Mark Latham of endangering the US alliance, and said Latham's policy on Iraq had given succour to terrorists and increased the risk to Australia. Especially at election time, John Howard wants us to think about our oxygen supply. And he wants us to think about the prospect of losing it under a Labor government.

The political use of fear is nothing new, of course. The father of conservatism, Edmund Burke, wrote that without fear, we are passive, but that fear is "the strongest emotion which the mind is capable of feeling". And Tocqueville, the French politician best remembered for his sharp-eyed appraisal of America, wrote in a note to himself that "Fear must be put to work on behalf of liberty."

Psychologists have demonstrated that people can be conditioned by fear to change their political behaviour. For instance, Jeff Greenberg of the University of Arizona and Sheldon Solomon of Skidmore College in New York State were able to get groups of 100 volunteers at a time to either endorse or reject George Bush's Iraq policy, depending on what subject the researchers asked them to think about immediately beforehand. "What we found was staggering," Greenberg said. When asked to think first about watching TV, people rejected Bush's policy in their next response. When asked to think about September 11, they endorsed it.

An Israeli psychologist, Daniel Kahneman, was the joint winner of the 2002 Nobel Prize in economic sciences for his work with Amos Tversky in developing prospect theory, which demonstrates the power of fear on human behaviour. They took issue with the dominant idea that humans are unerringly rational agents who seek to maximise their "utility function". By studying people's choices in placing hundreds of different bets, Tversky and Kahneman discovered that humans respond more strongly to the prospect of loss than to the possibility of gain. Indeed, they calculated that people dislike losses 225 per cent more than they like gains. In short, we humans are risk-averse, and will strive to prevent loss more energetically than we chase gain.

The implication of this for the last election is clear: Howard, by making us fear for our future prosperity and security, appealed to the stronger side of our nature than Latham, who played for our hopes and ambitions.

John Howard knows that we love the ANZUS Treaty. Over the decades, Australians have always supported its existence. Even during the darkest days of the Vietnam War, even in the midst of the US-led invasion and occupation of Iraq, even when Australians are strongly opposed to US policy, roughly two-thirds of us consistently tell pollsters that we favour our alliance with the US. This makes it one of the sacred cows of Australian political life. So Howard describes it as our security guarantee, knowing full well that there is no guarantee attached. Alan Renouf observes:

> He's a very astute politician and he reads the Australian electorate. We are lonely at this end of the earth, America is our great friend, it's very reassuring, and that's good politics, even if we will have become a cipher for the Americans.

Mark Latham ignored this to his cost. Latham tried to oppose the war in Iraq. He thought he was onto a winner – seven out of ten Australians disapproved of Australia's participation. But the moment he uttered the fateful phrase of wanting Australia's "troops home by Christmas", Howard outmanoeuvred him and framed it not as a question of Iraq but as an alliance issue. Latham would endanger the US alliance, said Howard. And George Bush concurred. This was so damaging to Latham that, by the time of the election campaign, he had stopped talking about it. It was a stunning piece of political maladroitness to contrive that, in the middle of an unpopular and ill-conceived war, the Opposition leader could not campaign on it.

For the 2007 election, Howard will use precisely the same approach. Already, he accuses Kevin Rudd of wanting to "rat on our allies". Once more, he will accuse Labor of trying to take away our great source of national reassurance, of leaving the Frightened Country alone and exposed on its "awkward slab of Europe" at the bottom of Asia.

In the face of our national anxiety, Howard represents the reassurance of the man in whose hands the alliance is safe – the hotline will be answered. From the moment he took office in 1996, it was one of his highest priorities to be seen to be the rightful owner of the US alliance, custodian of the national reassurance and father of our national security.

Kevin Rudd has written of the security partnership between the two countries:

> Both Labor and the Coalition had a part to play in establishing the alliance and can justifiably claim it as part of their foreign policy patrimony – Labor formed it in 1941 when John Curtin looked to America. The Liberals consummated it in 1951 when our wartime alliance became ANZUS. Labor has supported this alliance for sixty-five years – since before the Liberal Party was even born.

But in the mind of the Australian electorate, Labor has lost the alliance. John Howard has made it his. And with it, he has taken political possession of national security. The chairman of Newspoll, Sol Lebovic, says: "If you go back through the history of the polling, the peaks in John Howard's approval rating occurred during the guns incident [following the Port Arthur massacre], the Tampa affair and the terrorist attacks of September 11, the Bali bombing, and the war in Iraq."

If you doubt this, consider the action at the online betting shop Centrebet after a bomb went off in front of the Australian Embassy in Jakarta in September 2004. Overnight Centrebet saw an increase of 20 per cent on the total value of all election bets that the company had taken in the past year. The firm's manager, Gerard Duffy, reported that, "As soon as the news got out, we probably took $70,000 to $80,000 in bets for the Coalition." And what of new money on Labor's prospects? "We took half-a-dozen small – and I mean small – bets for less than $1000 total on Labor. So most punters out there think the election has firmed for the Coalition."

Has it changed? Today, as then, Australians say they trust the government, by a margin of two to one, as the better party to deal with national security. It is extraordinary but true that, in spite of the strategic disaster in Iraq bleeding and blasting its way across our TV screens for four years, Howard still holds such a strong grip on the claim to credibility on national security.

As Howard told the Coalition members' meeting on the first day of parliament in 2007, he will campaign on his strengths. The government still had the electorate's confidence on the issues that mattered to it, economic management and national security, he said. And that's where it would concentrate its efforts. Could this change? We saw in February that Howard's grip might be vulnerable. His attack on the US Democratic Party was ill-judged. He took aim at one of the party's star candidates for the presidency, Senator Barack Obama, for daring to propose a conditional, phased withdrawal of his own country's troops from Iraq. "If I were running Al Qaeda in Iraq, I would put a circle around March 2008 and be praying as many times as possible for a victory not only for Obama," said Howard, "but also for the Democrats."

This is bad alliance policy. America operates a two-party political system. Is it wise for an allied leader to alienate one of the two parties? Of course not. Not only does the Democratic Party control both chambers of the US Congress, but it may also control the White House after the 2008 election. And it's bad domestic politics. Because when Obama struck back, Howard was exposed. The American said:

> We have close to 140,000 troops on the ground now and my understanding is that Mr Howard has deployed 1400. So, if he's ginned up to fight the good fight in Iraq, I would suggest that he calls up

> another 20,000 Australians and sends them to Iraq, otherwise it's
> just a bunch of empty rhetoric.

This lent weight to the criticism that the Australian deployment is more political than military, more about posing as a big player than wanting to make a serious miltary contribution. As another former secretary of the Department of Foreign Affairs, Richard Woolcott, has said, "Our contribution is minimal and essentially symbolic." And it put Howard in a position where he was seen to be endangering bipartisan American support for Australia. It raises legitimate questions in the minds of the voting public: Can Howard only work with one half of the US political system? Is the alliance really safe in the hands of a man who puts partisan politics above the alliance? Howard quickly switched to put the onus onto Kevin Rudd to confess his true beliefs about the consequences of the withdrawal of US forces from Iraq.

The episode showed that Howard's judgment is imperfect, that his image as the custodian of the alliance could be vulnerable to challenge. Because the Australian public has seen Kevin Rudd on TV talking about foreign affairs for the past five years, he has already improved Labor's perceived standing on the subject of foreign policy. On the question of which party is better able to manage international relations, Rudd closed the deficit for Labor from twenty percentage points under Beazley to three, giving Labor near parity, according to the February ACNielsen poll. Still, Howard remained so far ahead on perceptions of competence on national security, defence and border protection that he would need to collapse into chronic misjudgment to surrender the government's commanding lead in the area. Rudd cannot seize this political trump card from the government, but Howard, through sustained political error or military catastrophe, could, just conceivably, hand it over.

John Howard frames each election as a referendum on economic management or national security or both. Even the new priority of global warming he is framing as a subset of competence in economic management. Kevin Rudd can see that he needs to capture these core credentials in his babushka doll set, but they are firmly in John Howard's possession and he has no intention of relinquishing them.

The Lucky Country finally started to make its own luck, and Howard has taken out a political monopoly on it. The Frightened Country still harbours dark anxieties, some old and some new. Howard, the necromancer of our national psyche, conjures our fears to frighten us, and then offers to banish them again to soothe us. He understands the Bipolar Nation.

Howard plans to use our luck and our fears, our hopes and our anxieties, as the basis for his fifth term, as he did with his second, third and fourth. If Kevin Rudd cannot wrest these powers from him in the months ahead, then Labor, gripped by its customary urge to self-mutilate in times of frustration, could once again come to resemble nothing so much as Bluey, a dog that Clive James once knew: "A known psychopath, Bluey would attack himself if nothing else was available. He used to chase himself in circles trying to bite his own balls off."

Eric Rolls

No Fixed Address is a fascinating and learned account of lives unknown to most of
us. During one remarkable stretch the reader lives with Robyn Davidson among
the nomads of Rajasthan. These are nomads by tradition and by their own nam-
ing. But I question her statement that "Traditionally oriented Aborigines are constantly on the move."

After years of working on *An Unknown People: Aboriginal Australians*, I hesitate to
call them "nomads" or even "hunter-gatherers". They were farmers by fire; they
managed the land to suit themselves but with absolute knowledge of the consequences of their actions. Even today the Gumatj people of Blue Mud Bay on the
western shores of the Gulf of Carpentaria extend the fruiting of cycads from
weeks to months by strategic firing. On Cape York, where the big game com-
prised eastern grey kangaroos in the south-east and agile wallabies in a wide
band around the whole coast, the people maintained paddocks of green grass
sprung by fire five to six kilometres apart because that is the distance kangaroos
move when they get a fright. Moreover, they remember where they got a fright,
especially when hunters made a good kill. So after the first succession of burns,
the managers staggered the next lot so that the kangaroos met good food instead
of unpleasant memories.

It is necessary to know how many people made such a wonderful job of
managing Australia. There are sufficient early figures available to reckon the
number who lived on the whole rich coastal strip from the Camden Haven
south of Port Macquarie to the Queensland border and from the coast west to
the Great Dividing Range. That 30,000 square kilometres nourished at least
60,000 people.

I cut out a rectangle of that size and applied it to areas of equal production on
the map of Australia. By suitable reduction of numbers in less favourable areas,
ending with one person per hundred square kilometres over a vast area of the

dry Centre, the total population before smallpox came to 1,500,000, with the probability that it was 2,500,000. Fewer people could not have maintained Australia as it was maintained. There was no wilderness. Every square metre of land, even in the really difficult places like the upper reaches of the Johnstone River in north Queensland, was known intimately.

Substantial numbers lived in beautiful permanent villages, especially those in present western Victoria who engaged in eel farming. The Gunditjmara people were the first fish farmers, beginning work in 6000 BC to grow short-finned eels (*Anguilla australis*), the principal eel of those waters and the best to eat. Before they began work, tidal Darlot Creek was fed by the Condah swamps, which were fed in turn from the overflow of Lake Condah. By a complex system of walls and trenches and dams, the people turned a big area into an eel farm. They enticed young eels in from the ocean and held them in the waterways and constructed dams for up to twenty years.

All this work required people constantly on the site. Since they had wall-building skills, they used them to build comfortable houses, laying the plentiful black, trapezoidal, basalt blocks in circular walls one metre high, then finishing off with a roof of bark or plaited reeds fitted to a timber frame. The remains of 175 houses have been found. Undoubtedly there were many more.

The first move in building the eel farm was to dam Darlot Creek with basalt blocks to give control of its water. Then, by building stone walls a metre high and more than fifty metres long, and digging channels a metre deep and nearly 300 metres long, they connected the lake, the swamp and the creek so that they could manipulate the water flow and with it the feed flow. Rainwater draining into the swamps brought important food for the eels and fish, so did every tide coming up the creek. None of it was easy work. The basalt blocks were heavy; the only digging tools were coolamons with fire-hardened cutting edges held by both hands.

Altogether they modified 10,000 hectares. The extended swamps and ponds that they created grew plants with edible roots and tubers; they attracted water-birds in thousands. They caught the eels and fish in woven cane traps placed in the maze of waterways. There was plenty to eat without much trouble getting it.

A rich society developed as soon as they had more eels than they could eat themselves. At the height of production the eels could have fed 10,000 people, about six times the number of those who grew them. So they smoked them for trade by cutting openings in the butt of hollow trees and hanging dressed eels inside over slow-burning smoky fires.

Word spread about the quality of the eels. People sought them from distant places, paying for them in goods that the Lake Condah people did not have: quartz, flint and stone axes, even spear-like wooden ornaments made from special woods in the Cape Otway ranges 200 kilometres away.

The Condah people also exported beautifully made possum-skin cloaks like those worn by their own lovely women. The cloaks were warm and they looked good.

A highly structured society developed at Lake Condah. Business, behaviour, life were controlled by several chiefs who had absolute control. They had four wives each; no common man was allowed more than one.

The Gunditjmara were not the only eel farmers. There was another system of traps at Lake Bolac on Salt Creek, an eastern tributary of the Hopkins River, 100 kilometres east-north-east of Lake Condah. The Jardwadjali people probably managed it. Up to a thousand people gathered there for a season of feasting and ceremony lasting from one to two months. As at Lake Condah the eels were principally short-finned eels, though there would have been a few less desirable long-finned eels among them at both places.

At Toolondo, south-west of Horsham in Victoria, the same people regulated the depth of water in swamps and made it easier to trap eels by joining two swamps with a ditch cut one metre deep, 2.5 metres wide and more than three kilometres long. They could cope with floods, they stored water in dry times. Near Mount William west of Ararat they put in six hectares of ditches. In a spell as Protector of Aborigines for New South Wales in the late 1830s, George Robinson described some of these works. He also mentioned many low weirs built of stone, sod or timber with circular holes in them to take plaited fish and eel traps. All these people lived settled lives.

The Wangkamana people on the strange, short Mulligan River in south-west Queensland led prosperous, settled lives as pituri farmers, a narcotic high in nicotine producing a drowsy sense of wellbeing. Not only were they the best growers of the plant, they had the best pituri to begin with. These people had so many resources that individuals specialised in their work. There were hereditary makers of canoes, shields, spears and boomerangs, hereditary fishermen, rain makers, medicine men, hunters, messengers, heralds, tree climbers. Among the women were yam hunters, basket makers, hut builders. Above all there were those who specialised in the cultivation and the packaging of the pituri. They carefully burnt off old growth to stimulate the production of new shoots, which produced the best pituri. They dried the narrow leaves over a fire, then pounded them with the ash of yarran (*Acacia omalophylla*), which, by a strange chemical change, freed the nicotine in the leaves when they were chewed.

They considered the packaging as much as a cigar maker displaying his cigars in an engraved wooden box. The most expert women wove bags out of coloured string wound from the common verbena (*Verbena officinalis*) that grew on the Diamantina and Georgina rivers and from broombush (*Melaleuca uncinata*) growing on sandhills. They dyed the string with red and yellow ochre and sometimes with the blue clay found in the Diamantina. They packed the leaves and ash tightly into the coloured bags. In times of plenty, the growers called neighbours to help with the picking. No doubt they paid them in pituri.

Up to five hundred people waited at Goyder Lagoon to buy the remarkable drug as carriers brought it down. Goyder Lagoon was one of the principal trading centres and hundreds of traders lived there for months at a time. That country is now so lonely and so remote that not even a track runs in there.

The Karuwali on the Diamantina River in western Queensland lived for long periods in solid, dome-shaped houses. They built a frame of coolibah branches lashed together with grass twine and kangaroo sinews, then covered it with layers of grass or spinifex mixed with wet sand. The final coating contained spinifex gum. When this layer dried, the outer surface was brick hard. Walls and roof were 25 to 30 centimetres thick, making them cool in summer and warm in winter. Alice Duncan-Kemp, author of *Where Strange Paths Go Down*, who knew the people, considered that these houses were more impervious to rain and high winds than some early white homesteads.

There is an old song, one of the world's great poems, in northern Arnhem Land called "The Goulburn Island Cycle". It begins, as most songs do, with establishing the site, building the atmosphere. They are preparing for the wet season, encouraging the storm clouds, by building their wet-season homes. Some are built to float and are tied like swans' nests in the lagoon that is on the mainland opposite the Goulburn Islands. The majority are solid two-storey constructions. The stringy-bark roofs are spread with a slurry of termite mounds that is forced between the overlaps. It dries hard and waterproof.

The poem is thousands of lines long. Here is how it begins:

> Erecting forked sticks and rafters, posts for the floor, making the
> roof of the hut like a sea-eagle's nest:
>> They are always there, at the billabong of the goose eggs, at the
>> wide expanse of water.
>> As they build, they think of the monsoon rains – rain and wind
>> from the west, clouds spreading over the billabong …

For a time, after good rain, the people who lived in the dry Centre became hunter-gatherers. They usually lived at wells or spring-fed waterholes, or at dams that they constructed to catch runoff from hills. They also diverted water to irrigate favoured grasses. They walked along the sides of sandhills throwing out grass seed from little emu-skin bags sewn with sinews from kangaroo tails. They burnt small areas to keep *Solanum* growing happily.

They built accommodation that suited the climate and the general conditions. There was little timber for building so they surrounded basins scooped in the sand with balls of spinifex (*Triodia spp.*) tangled together in several rows. The spinifex walls gave good protection from the sand that often blew in uncomfortable storms.

The rain gave them the opportunity to spread in small groups over a wide area and spell the animals and plants that had supported them for months. When the new waters gave out, the plants began to die and the animals to vanish, they came back to the stable waters and a settled life. Always they stored surplus food.

A.C. Gregory, on Coopers Creek in search of Leichhardt in 1858, reported that:

> the natives reap a panicum grass. Fields of 1000 acres [400 hectares] are there met with growing this cereal. The natives cut it down by means of stone knives, cutting down the stalk halfway, beat out the seed, leaving the straw which is often met with in large heaps.

One man reported seeing sixty Aborigines engaged in harvesting seeds. Most people harvested all the seed they could while it was available, then stored the surplus in kangaroo-skin bags and wooden dishes about 30 centimetres deep and 1.5 metres long. Stores of a tonne of grain were reported.

Aboriginal Australians as the first bakers, the first astronomers, the first fish farmers, the first artists, the first historians, the first people to form strong religious beliefs, the creators of great poetry are unknown to the majority of Australians.

Eric Rolls

Kate Grenville

I'm a great admirer of Inga Clendinnen's writing and found *The History Question* full of the insights and thoughtfulness that characterise all her work. She spends some time discussing *The Secret River*, and I'm glad of the opportunity to make a few comments about that aspect of her essay.

Clendinnen isn't the only historian to think that I regard *The Secret River* as history, and that I claim for it the authority of history: Mark McKenna (mentioned by Clendinnen in her essay) led the charge with his "Writing the Past", published in the *Australian Financial Review* on 16 December 2005. (A revised version of this essay appears in *Best Australian Essays* 2006, ed. Drusilla Modjeska, Black Inc., Melbourne, 2006.)

Clendinnen paraphrases McKenna's argument when she says, "Grenville discovered she could write history after all. The novel is a serious attempt to do history ... Grenville sees her novel as a work of history." Although Clendinnen gives no source for this claim, it could well have come from McKenna's piece, so in this reply I'll refer to his essay as well as hers.

Both McKenna's essay and Clendinnen's quote me as claiming to have written history — and in fact to have written better history than historians. However, the quotes that they use have been narrowly selected, taken out of context, and truncated. They don't represent what I actually think. But, like Chinese Whispers, those "quotes" are now being quoted by others — and for this reason I'd like to put the record straight.

Here it is in plain words: I don't think *The Secret River* is history — it's a work of fiction. Like much fiction, it had its beginnings in the world, but those beginnings have been adapted and altered to various degrees for the sake of the fiction.

Nor did I ever *say* that I thought my novel was history. In fact, on countless occasions I was at pains to make it clear that I knew it wasn't.

Perhaps the most accessible of these sources is the Acknowledgments in the back of the book itself, containing this statement:

> One of my ancestors gave me the basis for certain details in the early life of William Thornhill, and other characters share some qualities with historical figures. All the people within these pages, however, are works of fiction.
>
> In the course of research I consulted countless documents ... and adapted them for my imaginative purposes. Readers of, for example, the Old Bailey transcripts for 1806, or the Governor's dispatches from early Sydney, may recognise a few lines. I acknowledge with gratitude the work of others in making such resources available to a writer of fiction.

(By these "others", of course, I mainly meant historians.)

On my website (updated with this material in August 2005 and hard to miss on Google) I went into more detail about what I thought I'd done:

> This book isn't history, but it's solidly based on history. Most of the events in the book "really happened" and much of the dialogue is what people really said or wrote.
>
> Whenever possible I based events in the book on recorded historical events, adapting and changing them as necessary. Thornhill's first meeting with the Aboriginal people on the Hawkesbury is based on a similar incident involving the first Governor, Captain Arthur Phillip. The incident in which Captain McCallum fails to ambush a group of Aboriginal people is based on many accounts of similar failures by the military. The Proclamation which gives settlers permission to shoot Aboriginal people is taken verbatim from Governor Macquarie's Proclamation of 1816. The massacre scene is based on eyewitness accounts of the Waterloo Creek killings in 1838.
>
> Some characters are also loosely based on historical figures, and some of their dialogue is taken from their own mouths ... [There follow some examples of this.]
>
> It was important to me that the incidents and characters were solidly based on history, but as a novelist I drew on these historical sources loosely, as a starting-point for the work of the imagination.

> The final events and characters meld many historical references together – they're fiction, but they're based on fact.

I'm sorry that my adaptation of historical sources has caused Inga Clendinnen to "flinch" – but it's what fiction writers do: take the world and modify it. I've always made it clear, though, that I *have* modified it. I've spelled out my awareness that I'm writing fiction, not history.

Of course, it would have been simpler to answer all questions about The Secret River in the way Clendinnen describes Peter Carey doing when interviewed about The True History of the Kelly Gang: by saying flatly, unanswerably: "I made it up."

But I was interested in trying to do something a little more nuanced than that: to acknowledge the complex relationship, backwards and forwards across an invisible line, between the world of fiction and the world inhabited by living people. In talking about the book in public, I was trying to describe my own journey around that line.

There are plenty of easily accessible sources, then, for historians to consult in order to find out what I thought I was doing in The Secret River. But these aren't the sources Clendinnen, or McKenna, has chosen to quote. Instead, they use a few newspaper stories and a radio interview.

Better than most, historians would know that conclusions are only as reliable as the sources on which they're based. They would be aware, too, of the limitations of the kinds of sources they've used.

First, the context of these interviews: readers (and thus interviewers for book pages and programs) are interested in the fiction-making process and often want to know "Where do you get your ideas?" For an historical novel, they also want to know "How much of it is based on fact?" In other words, the context of my remarks was always that of a writer of fiction answering the question "How did you write this novel?" My answer was that I wasn't writing history, but I wasn't inventing incidents and details out of thin air, either.

In interviews I explained, much as I did on my website, quoted above, that I'd taken events from the historical record and shifted their time and place, and that I'd ascribed to one man things that were actually done by another man. I told audiences the different dates, I spelled out the different locations. I made it clear that I'd used the historical record, but that I'd freely adapted it for my purposes, and that although many of the events I describe "really happened", they didn't happen to a man called William Thornhill in 1816, because he's a fictional construction. In dozens of interviews I was scrupulous in making a distinction between what's described in the historical record and how I'd departed from it.

One of these interviews was with Ramona Koval, in a program quoted by Clendinnen. I talked about the "experiential research" I did in order to write *The Secret River*, and how I used empathy – "What would I have done in that situation?" – to try to construct characters. Clendinnen suggests that this is very poor history, because "Grenville would not have been Grenville in that situation."

I agree – this would be poor history indeed. But these weren't the comments of someone claiming to be doing history and describing how she went about historical research. The context for my remarks about empathy was that Koval had asked me to read a passage from the novel, which included mention of "thole-pins" (an old form of rowlocks). Our conversation began with her inviting me to talk about that aspect of the novel: "I think anybody listening to that must be particularly impressed with the language and the technicalities of the work of the lighterman turned sailor, I suppose, in the colonies. How did you find these ways to express this kind of work?" In other words, this wasn't a question about how to write history: it was a question to a novelist about how she'd written her work of fiction. The context of my remarks about empathy – to which Clendinnen takes such exception – wasn't that of someone explaining how they did history, but someone explaining how they did fiction.

A significant limitation of interviews as a reliable source for debate is that interviews are made on the run. Even politicians, those masters of the one-liner, have been known to get it wrong under those conditions. How much more will writers, who often became writers in the first place because they're not particularly quick on their feet?

Clendinnen (and McKenna before her) quotes from the same radio interview, in which I used the now-infamous "stepladder" image. Their reading of this extract is that I'm claiming a superiority for fiction over history: that fiction is "further up the ladder".

As her final question that day, with the ABC clock sweeping towards the end of our time in our separate studios, Ramona asked me: "So where would you put your book, finally, if you were laying out books on the history wars? Whereabouts would you slot yours?" With Windschuttle and Reynolds – the massacre denialists and the massacre acknowledgers – in the front of my mind, I answered:

> Mine would be up on a ladder, looking down at the history wars. [The website transcript of this is "looking down *on* the history wars" but the audio is clearly "*at*" – a small but significant distinction.] I think the historians, and rightly so, have battled away about

the details of exactly when and where and how many and how much, and they've got themselves into these polarised positions, and that's fine, I think that's what historians ought to be doing: constantly questioning the evidence and perhaps even each other. But a novelist can stand up on a stepladder and look down at this, *outside the fray*, [emphasis in original audio] and say there is another way to understand it ... That's what I hope this book will be. It stands outside that polarised conflict and says look, this is a problem we really need, as a nation, to come to grips with. The historians are doing their thing, but let me as a novelist come to it in a different way, which is the way of empathising and imaginative understanding of those difficult events. Basically to think, well, what would I have done in that situation, and what sort of a person would that make me?

Written down and read in cold blood, and without the extra dimension given by tone of voice, this certainly ain't Einstein. But I think it's clear that the stepladder image wasn't being used to imply superiority. The concept I was reaching for was to do with being different from the historians, perched up high on a removed vantage point where I could watch, but not be involved. My book – because it's a novel – is outside the "history wars", irrelevant to them. As a novelist, I'm just an interested onlooker who made the mistake of climbing a stepladder rather than a couple of fruit boxes to get a good view.

I think that comes through pretty unmistakably, but I recognise that the stepladder image might be seen to contain an ambiguity I didn't intend. If I'd been quietly sitting at my desk writing (and then revising at leisure) for *Quarterly Essay*, I'd have used a different one. However, there's no chance to revise on air.

The fact that this quickly grabbed image is the one that's being used again and again by historians indicates that this is the only support they can muster for their claim that I think fiction is superior to history. It strikes me as a pretty flimsy support for such a large claim.

Let me go on record now as saying that I don't think – and never have thought – that fiction is superior to history, much less that my own novel is superior to the work of historians.

In his essay "Writing the Past", Mark McKenna seems to have been the one to initiate the idea that I claim to be writing history rather than fiction – an idea that Clendinnen then extends. In support of this argument McKenna quotes the "stepladder" image from the Ramona Koval interview, plus a few stories written for daily newspapers. These are feature pieces and news stories by journalists incorporating brief quotes or paraphrased remarks from me. They're not verbatim transcripts, they don't contain extended quotes, and I didn't see them before publication.

However, these sketchy and partial quotes and paraphrases are the only evidence that McKenna has produced for his claim that I think my novel is history. This is the claim that Clendinnen repeats when she says "Grenville sees her novel as a work of history." Those newspaper stories are being asked to bear a burden which they were never intended to bear – to accurately represent my views on a complex subject.

This is by no means to criticise those journalists or their stories. It's to recognise the limitation of the form itself and its context as an ephemeral piece for a daily paper. The problem is not in the pieces themselves, but in the fact that they've been used inappropriately – they've been taken uncritically, at face value, as authoritative evidence.

Much more accurate, considered material was easily available – for example the long piece on my website. I'm surprised that historians are basing such an important argument on these newspaper stories while other sources – ones that give a very different view – are being ignored.

I've also been surprised by the scornful, mocking tone of the historians' discussions of *The Secret River*. Historians have every right to doubt the value of historical fiction, and to dislike any particular example of it. But personalising the discussion seems to go beyond a fruitful debate about the roles of history and fiction.

I recently heard an interview with Amanda Lohrey in which she mentioned her dislike for historical fiction because it's "bogus", and next day I read Henry James' comments in a similar vein, as quoted by Clendinnen. I share much of their distrust of historical fiction and am as uncomfortable as they are with the sleight of hand used by the historical novelist.

In fact, *The Secret River* started life not as an historical novel but as a book of non-fiction – I'd planned a kind of loose biography of my convict ancestor. When I realised – for various reasons and with some dismay – that I was writing an historical novel, I came up with a way of reconciling myself to my uneasiness about that genre. I decided to write a second book to accompany the novel: one in which I'd show where the history ended and the fiction began in *The Secret River* – a record of the writing process, and of the thinking that lay behind it. Rather than hiding behind the sleight of hand of the novelist, I'd try to make the process transparent (in the same way I later attempted to do in interviews).

So, concurrently with the novel, I worked on that second book, which has now been published: *Searching for the Secret River*.

It's a book in which I've tried to explore something of what happens when the novelist's imagination works on the world around them — a world which includes history and historical sources. Readers often ask novelists, "Is your work autobiographical?" and most novelists hate the question because the answer can be both yes and no. Teasing out the nuances of the yes-ness and the no-ness is a complicated business. In *Searching for the Secret River*, I've tried to do a similar kind of teasing-out about sources, and to acknowledge both my debt to history (and historians) and the ways I've departed from it, and why.

Clendinnen opens her chapter on *The Secret River* with the image of history and fiction jogging along together on adjacent tracks in an amicable way. Now, she says, novelists "have been doing their best to bump historians off the track". I've never wished to challenge historians' right to their track, and I've always assumed that their footing on it was, in any case, unshakably secure.

In my view, novelists are just doing what we've always done — taking aspects of the world and turning them into stories — and are taking up much the same space on the tracks that we always have. There are many and varied tracks back into the past, and my feeling is that there's plenty of room on them for all of us.

Kate Grenville

Inga Clendinnen

I'm sorry Kate Grenville feels misrepresented. I fretted, briefly, about analysing even a transcript interview – strange things can happen in interviews – but this one came late in an intense promotional campaign for the novel, when Grenville had presumably decided what she most wanted to say. She certainly spoke with exuberant confidence. After acknowledging Koval's praise for the depth and detail of her historical research, she declared her subject to be "the white settler response to the fact that the Aboriginal people were on the land they wanted to settle on", because "until we are prepared to look at all those slightly hidden, slightly secret places in our history, we can't actually make much progress into the future." I took this to be a claim to be writing history, while writing fiction as well. But now we have *Searching for the Secret River*, Grenville's account of how a family history transformed into a novel, where she is prepared to have what she says taken seriously. In what follows I will focus on the issue of context to demonstrate why so many historians believe so few novelists are capable of illuminating the actual past.

Grenville's initial intention had been to write the history of her convict ancestor Solomon Wiseman. Then she decided to change heroes in, as it were, midstream, from the "real" but frustratingly enigmatic Wiseman to an invented and therefore marvellously amenable character called William Thornhill (*Searching for the Secret River*, pp. 185–6). She believed that decision liberated her from the confusions and opacities of the ascertainable record and allowed her to construct a telling story, but a story which remained broadly faithful to the documentary record:

> By rearranging and reshaping the scenes ... I could create a sequence. That wasn't quite how it was in the documents, but making a sequence out of these events wouldn't distort what had "really happened" in any significant way. It would, though, turn them into a story ... (*SSR*, p. 185).

A little later:

> I was shameless in rifling through research for anything I could use,
> wrenching it out of its place and adapting it for my own purposes
> … but I was trying to be faithful to the shape of the historical
> record, and the meaning of all those events historians had written
> about. What I was writing wasn't real, but it was as true as I could
> make it (SSR, p. 191).

"Wrenching"? "Adapting"? And instantly historians' hackles are up. If we are
to begin to understand what individuals might once have been up to, it is essential to reflect not only on what they did or failed to do, but also on the context
– physical, social, political, cultural – in which they did or failed to do it. We
have to realise that our subjects' understanding of their situation is likely to be
different from our own and will certainly change through time, as they themselves will change through time and the accumulation of experience. Otherwise
we make them unchanging chessmen on a fixed chessboard.

To take one episode which both Grenville and I find compelling, for very different reasons: the Curious Incident of the Old Man and the Spade. The event so
captivates Grenville that in *Searching for the Secret River* she quotes Governor Phillip's
account of what happened very nearly in full, so saving me the trouble (see SSR,
pp. 111–12). This is my account of the meanings to be discovered in that small
episode.

From the first days of contact there had been tense but surprisingly genial
encounters between the British intruders and the local residents in the bays and
beaches around Port Jackson (I describe them in *Dancing with Strangers*), but the
great physical fact of the settlement itself had been ignored. It was only six
weeks after the British disembarkation that two old Aboriginal men came into
view, sat down a little distance from the camp, accepted a few presents (yellow
tinfoil, red bunting, a hatchet), and after about an hour of this got up and
walked away, all without saying a word: a glimpse of the stately pace of Aboriginal diplomacy when dealing with strangers.

Only a week before, in a different place, Phillip had had a very different experience. At the beginning of March 1788 he and a small party had set out to
explore the area we now call Broken Bay. The first couple of days were spent
exploring the northern arm, where they came across several groups of Aboriginal men, women and children. The men were armed and watchful, but suffi-
ciently affable. Then late on the third day the British boats entered the southern

arm of the bay. They had a hard time getting around the headland, only to find the "sheltered" water dangerously shallow, but an old man who was standing with a youth on a rocky outcrop guided them carefully to shore, where he welcomed them with a gift of fire. Then he led a couple of the officers to the entrance of a cave and gestured for them to go in. Being British officers and therefore sensibly cautious, they refused; it rained all night; everyone got miserably wet. The next morning they found the cave was quite big enough to have kept the lot of them snug and dry.

When Phillip and his boats returned two days later, the old man was again waiting, and this time he greeted them with "a song and a dance of joy". And the historian is transfixed. Contrast that joyful dance with the silent aloofness of the Aboriginal delegation to the settlement. This old man must think he knows who the strangers are. He watched for their first coming, stationed himself to receive them, treated them with hostly warmth. They come back; he greets them with his "song and dance of joy". This suggests that he not only "recognises" them, but that he believes the recognition to be mutual – that they will be able to "read" the dance.

Phillip, suspecting none of this but touched by the display of warmth, presented the old man with a hatchet and some other small gifts. Then, "when it was dark", says Phillip,

> he stole a spade, and was caught in the fact. I thought it necessary to show I was displeased with him, and therefore when he came to me, pushed him away, and gave him two or three slight slaps on the shoulder with the open hand, at the same time pointing to the spade.

"This", Phillip remembers, "destroyed our friendship in a moment": the old man grabbed up a spear, advanced on Phillip, threatened to throw; Phillip remained steadfast; the old man lowered his spear – and Phillip was persuaded a valuable trans-cultural moral lesson had been taught: thou shalt not steal.

Grenville admits she is puzzled by the incident (SSR, pp. 111–12). If the old man had wanted the spade so much, why didn't he take the trouble to steal it more deftly? And why didn't he spear Phillip? The historian asks: was this "theft" at all? Phillip, drenched with the notion of the sanctity of individual property, thought it was. But the old man? All we know is that he picks the spade up. Does he assume he has a right to it? And then, despite the insult of the gratuitous physical assault (we know from the touchiness of even the "gentle" Arabanoo that for the Aboriginal male the person was the site of honour) the old man lowers his spear. Why? Does "Phillip"– or whoever it is he takes Phillip to be – stand within a protected relationship? Is it not possible for him to spear him?

What does Grenville do with this marvellous moment? First she uses those schoolteacherly slaps as evidence of Phillip's propensity for violence when challenged: "Only a short time later, back in the settlement, the governor's convict gamekeeper, McEntire, was speared … [and] this time Phillip sent a party of soldiers out" (SSR, p. 112). For my very different reading of the two punitive expeditions, with the most bloodthirsty instructions and not the least result, see *Dancing with Strangers* chapter 18. But for the moment my quarrel is not with the interpretation, but with that brisk collapsing of time: "only a short time later". Phillip had his meeting with the old man in March 1788 within five weeks of landfall. The gamekeeper McEntire was speared on 9 December 1790. Thirty months apart. A world of things had happened between Aborigines and British since the old man's dance of joy: the kidnapping of Arabanoo, the smallpox, Baneelon's captivity, Phillip's spearing; then the peaceful invasion and repossession of the British settlement by local Aborigines. Only then McEntire is speared. By then, Phillip had become a different man, and was responding to a different set of prompts in a different situation.

Grenville makes her major use of the spade-and-slapping episode elsewhere. She bestows it on her fictional character Thornhill 30 kilometres upriver from the original site – and twenty-five years of bitter experience later. As she puts it:

> I adapted from other sources, giving to Wiseman the meeting between Governor Phillip and the "old man" at Broken Bay, for example. I adapted loosely, but kept the basic shape of the encounter, and especially the piercing detail of the "three slight slaps" (SSR, p. 162).

"The basic shape of the encounter." In fact Grenville keeps only an ugly tussle over a spade in an atmosphere of mutual incomprehension, three slaps delivered by Thornhill, and (in her freehand fictional version) three vigorous slaps returned by a younger Aboriginal man. The "basic shape" is gone, along with the "song and dance of joy" – and along with the inspiriting mystery.

Grenville is determined to respect the "otherness" of Aborigines. She therefore refuses to bestow upon them anything beyond a compelling physical presence and an indestructible nobility. This means she must deny her Aborigines the capacity to learn. Yet Aborigines and whites had been in sometimes friendly, sometimes abrasive contact along the Hawkesbury since 1791, with routes for the dissemination of information open well before that, and blacks traded reports at least as eagerly as whites. Grenville's Aborigines bear not the least resemblance to the information-hungry, brilliantly adaptive people I kept meeting in the British texts. There we can see speculations, experiments and strategies for managing the pallid intruders being accumulated, tested, exchanged. For men of their experience and situation, Grenville's Aborigines know far too little about white men and how to manage them. They are, therefore, sitting ducks.

Nonetheless – when Grenville says "I was shameless in rifling through research for anything I could use, wrenching it out of its place and adapting it for my own purposes," historians might blench, but most readers won't. *The Secret River* is selling well, and people who would never read a history book are learning something about our past from it. But I want non-historians to understand historians' apparent churlishness when faced with Grenville's insouciant exploitation of fragments of the past. Historians have a professional obligation to preserve documented moments surviving from the past as entirely as we are able because such moments are precious, and fragile. They must somehow make their way into the written record, and then be preserved long enough for a practised intelligence to mine them for meanings. Phillip, that most unusual conqueror, bothered to record, in detail, a fleeting contretemps with a naked old man: an episode as trivial to Phillip's superiors as it was to most of Phillip's companions. We have it only by unusual good luck. Yet with that little sequence of action properly contexted – with time, persons and place respected – we are privileged to see something we would otherwise never have seen. Such moments are too rare for us to watch them dismembered and rearranged to meet some private purpose. It is like watching a sandpiper's nest stumbled upon, casually looted, and the eggs broken to make a breakfast omelette. Grenville needs to modify her summary statement: "What I was writing wasn't true. It was, however, as real as I could make it."

I set novelists who claim to illuminate the past high standards, but those standards are sometimes met. Penelope Fitzgerald meets, even surpasses them in her novel *The Blue Flower*. Fitzgerald also knows exactly what she is doing, as she demonstrates by her choice of epigraph, which she takes from the writings of the novel's young hero Fritz von Hardenberg before he became "Novalis", Prophet of Early German Romanticism. It runs: "Novels arise out of the shortcomings of history."

Inga Clendinnen

Inga Clendinnen is a distinguished historian of the Spanish encounters with Aztec and Maya Indians of sixteenth-century America. Her *Reading the Holocaust* was named a *New York Times* best book of the year and awarded the NSW Premier's General History Award in 1999. Clendinnen's ABC Boyer Lectures, *True Stories*, were published in 2000, as was her award-winning memoir, *Tiger's Eye*. In 2003 *Dancing with Strangers* attracted wide critical acclaim. Her latest book is *Agamemnon's Kiss: Selected Essays*.

Kate Grenville's novel *The Secret River* won the 2006 Commonwealth Writers' Prize, the Christina Stead Prize for Fiction, and was shortlisted for the 2006 Man Booker Prize. *Searching for the Secret River* was published in 2006. Her other works of fiction are *Lilian's Story*, *Dreamhouse*, *Joan Makes History*, *Dark Places* and *The Idea of Perfection*.

Peter Hartcher is the political and international editor for the *Sydney Morning Herald* and was until 2004 the Washington bureau chief of the *Australian Financial Review*. In 1996, he received the Gold Walkley Award. He is the author of two books, *The Ministry* and *Bubble Man*, and a visiting fellow at the Lowy Institute for International Policy.

Eric Rolls was born in 1925 and brought up in northern New South Wales. He is the author of many highly praised books, including *A Million Wild Acres*, *Sojourners*, *Australia: A Biography* and *Celebration of the Senses*. His forthcoming book is *An Unknown People: Aboriginal Australians*.

www.ingramcontent.com/pod-product-compliance
Lightning Source LLC
Chambersburg PA
CBHW061224270326
41927CB00025B/3490